The
Water Mysteries
of Mesa Verde

The
Water Mysteries
of Mesa Verde

Kenneth R. Wright

Johnson Books

BOULDER

Published by Johnson Books, a division of Big Earth Publishing, 3005 Center Green Drive, Suite 220, Boulder, Colorado 80301. E-mail: books@bigearthpublishing.com www.johnsonbooks.com

Cover design: shushudesign
Cover photo: Gary Witt
Composition: Eric Christensen

9 8 7 6 5 4 3 2 1

Library of Congress Cataloging-in-Publication Data
Wright, Kenneth R.
    The Water Mysteries of Mesa Verde / Kenneth R. Wright
        p. cm.
    Includes bibliographical references.
    ISBN 1-55566-380-X
    1. Pueblo Indians—Colorado—Mesa Verde National Park—Antiquities. 2. Pueblo Indians—Agriculture—Colorado—Mesa Verde National Park. 3. Irrigation engineering, Prehistoric—Colorado—Mesa Verde National Park. 4. Irrigation farming—Colorado—Mesa Verde National Park. 5. Water-supply—Colorado—Mesa Verde National Park. 6. Reservoirs—Colorado—Mesa Verde National Park. 7. Excavations (Archaeology)—Colorado—Mesa Verde National Park. 8. Paleohydrology—Colorado—Mesa Verde National Park. 9. Mesa Verde National Park (Colo.)—Antiquities. I. Title
    E99.P9W76 2006
    978.8'27—dc22   2006005664

Printed in the United States of America

Contents

Foreword

FIVE HUNDRED YEARS before the Indians discovered Columbus; six hundred years before horses escaping Mexico reached the Four Corners region of Utah, Arizona, New Mexico, and Colorado; eight hundred years before Franciscans from Santa Fe camped below table bluffs the Spanish called Mesa Verde; nine hundred years before a cowboy chasing a stray reported a castle-like "city of stone" preserved like a fly in amber; and one thousand years before Congress made the mesa a national park in 1906, prehistoric farmers sustained a thriving civilization in the Four Corners region and transformed an American mesa through remarkable public works.

Archaeologists sometimes call them "Anasazi." We know them as Ancestral Puebloans. Monuments to their genius remain in cliffside apartment houses, conical turrets and watchtowers, terraced fields with check dams, pit-house sanctuaries with circular chambers (*kivas* in the Hopi language), and ruins of a medieval road system. Why did they leave? Where did they go? Although archaeologists hotly debate the reasons for the demise of the Ancestral Puebloans, Kenneth R. Wright of Denver, a civil engineer, probes the technology behind their success. How, he asks, did people get drinking water? How, on a riverless mesa where infrequent rains flashed through gullies and vanished, soaking through porous ground, did the ancients find enough water to supply a population that rivaled that which lives near the mesa today?

Clouds drag shadows across a sagebrush-juniper canyon. A bull snake disappears through the bed of an ancient canal. "A typical Mesa Verde ditch," says Wright. Dressed like his picture in *National Geographic*—white linen shirt and pants, fleece vest, gray boots—Wright is mapping the point where the canal intercepted a creek. Surveyors triangulate. A Park Service archaeologist wades through a trash heap of animal bones and potsherds. Nearby, on a flattish mound—once, according to Wright, a pool of drinking water—hardworking colleagues core soil with a jackhammer drill. "Maybe it began with a hole in the streamside," Wright continues. "Maybe they dug 10 feet or more before water was encountered in the hole. They scooped out the hole with sticks and baskets. Because it was such hard work after operations began, they never dug it out entirely. Maybe the reservoir floor grew an inch or two per year. Every time the floor rose, they had to elevate and extend the canal." Wright pauses and draws from his pipe. "People think these Indians were just running around in loincloths. It took work to maintain this system—work and organization. The Ancestral Puebloans maintained some of these systems for hundreds of years."

A native of Wisconsin who joined the Bureau of Reclamation before venturing out on his own in the dawn of the Kennedy years, Wright sees connections between perseverance and quality work. At Peru's Machu Picchu, sacred city of the Inca rulers, bureaucrats made him wait twenty years for a permit to study the ancient hydraulics. Patience and gentle diplomacy at last secured the permit in 1994. Together with Ruth Wright—his wife, a photographer and also an attorney who served fourteen years in the Colorado Legislature, six as minority leader of the House of Representatives—Ken founded the Wright Paleohydrological Institute for the study of ancient construction. Seven years later the institute completed what *National Geographic* has called "invaluable … the most detailed map ever made of Machu Picchu." In 2001 the American Society of Civil Engineers awarded the investigation its history and heritage prize.

Likewise, at Mesa Verde the Wrights persevere, still applying for permits, still contesting the conclusions drawn by entrenched experts. For decades Mesa Verde scholars scoffed at the theory that reservoirs had been constructed in the area. Some experts thought the flat little hill in Morefield Canyon might have been a dance platform, an erosional remnant, or perhaps just an odd little mound. But an excavated sample of silt with traces of iron oxide showed contact with standing water. Now even those who previously were skeptics are convinced that the national park has four—and possibly two more yet untested—prehistoric reservoir sites. The Colorado Historical Society provided four research grants to Wright and gave him the Stephen Hart Award for his research, and in 2004 the American Society of Civil Engineers dedicated the four reservoir sites as a National Historic Civil Engineering Landmark.

American Public Works Association's massively comprehensive *History of Public Works in the United States* (1976) flatly maintained that "the first American waterworks" was the wooden reservoir in Bethlehem, Pennsylvania, completed in 1754. Mesa Verde's canal-fed Morefield Reservoir, with its 120,000-gallon storage capacity, easily trumps Bethlehem's wooden structure. And although fire has long since destroyed colonial Bethlehem, and the famous steelworks there have long since stopped making steel, the Ancestral Puebloans maintained their site in Morefield Canyon for approximately 350 years. Longevity—not just efficiency—is the hallmark of good engineering. Wright reminds us that infrastructure predates asphalt and superhighways, that builders in all places and times have innovated in order to cope with harsh environments, that humans have been highly technological creatures since they first mastered the opposable thumb. Wright takes us back to basics. His research revisits a time before the pace of modern invention so quickly made things obsolete.

Todd Shallat, historian
Boise, Idaho

Acknowledgments

This book on Mesa Verde prehistoric reservoirs is dedicated to two groups of reservoir researchers to whom I owe much. The first group is made up of the past and present archaeologists, who have helped make Mesa Verde understandable and relevant to the public.

- David Breternitz
- Frederick H. Chapin
- Mona Charles
- Susan Collins
- Calvin Cummings
- Jesse W. Fewkes
- Harold S. Gladwin
- Alden Hayes
- Bonnie Hildebrand
- James Kleidon
- James A. Lancaster
- Sean Larmore
- Robert H. Lister
- George McLellan
- Earl Morris
- Kara Naber
- Larry Nordby
- Gustaf Nordenskiold
- Arthur Rohn
- Jeri Smalley
- Jack Smith
- Linda Towle
- Guy Stewart
- Joe Ben Wheat
- Cynthia Williams
- Richard Woodbury
- Don G. Wyckoff
- Ezra Zubrow

The second group is made of up of the professionals and technicians who joined me in the field or office over the ten-year period of the Mesa Verde research to help ferret out the on-the-ground truth and facts related to the ancient reservoirs and the hardworking Ancestral Puebloans who built and operated them.

- Jason Alexander, Water Resources Engineer
- David Baysinger, Video Production, Denver Museum of Natural History
- Eric Bikis, Hydrogeologist
- Aurora Bouchier, Geologist
- Chris Brown, GIS Specialist
- Ted Brown, Water Resources Engineer
- Melissa Churchill, Archaeological Technician

- Chris Crowley, Forest Hydrologist
- Linda Scott Cummings, Palynologist
- Owen Davis, Palynologist
- T. Andrew Earles, Hydrologist
- John Ewy, Civil Engineer
- Elizabeth Fassman, Hydrologist
- Peter Foster, Civil Engineer
- David Foss, Environmental Engineer
- Michael Frachetti, Archaeological Graphics
- Matt Gavin, Civil Engineer
- Mary Gillam, Quaternary Geologist
- Brad Hagen, Civil Engineer
- Bobbie Hobbs, Photographer
- Gregory Hobbs, Justice, Colorado Supreme Court
- Richard Holloway, Palynologist
- Robert Houghtalen, Hydraulic Engineer, Professor, Rose-Hulman Institute of Technology
- Robert Jarrett, Paleoflood Hydrologist, U.S. Geological Survey
- Lisa Klapper, Civil Engineer
- Sally Kribs, Technical Editor
- Bastiaan Lammers, Water Resources Technician
- Tom Langan, Hydrologist
- Peter Laux, Geologist
- Charles Lawler, Hydrologist
- Kurt Loptien, Geologist
- William Lorah, Hydraulic Engineer
- Rita Lovato, Video Producer
- Scott Marshall, Civil Engineer
- Gordon McEwan, Scientific Advisor, former Curator New World Department, Denver Art Museum
- David Mehan, Forest Hydrologist
- Peter Monkmeyer, Professor, University of Wisconsin
- John O'Brien, Climatologist
- Ernie Pemberton, Sedimentation Engineer
- Rachel Pittinger, Environmental Engineer
- Patricia Pinson, Archivist
- Maria Prokop, Water Resource Technician, U.S. Bureau of Reclamation
- Douglas Ramsey, Soils Scientist, U.S. Natural Resources Conservation Service
- Shannon Richardson, Field Technician
- John Rold, Colorado State Geologist (Retired)
- Lynette Shaper, Water Resources Engineer
- Janice Sheftel, Water Resources Attorney
- Terri Shelefontiuk, Administrator/Archivist
- Mary Simmerman, Word Processing
- Donald Tucker, Archaeological Technician
- Jean Tucker, Archaeological Technician

- Ryan Unterreiner, Biological Scientist/Surveyor
- Linda VanDamme, Water Resources Technician
- Robin VerSchneider, Geologist
- Kim Warhoe, CAD Specialist
- Rose Wallick, Water Resource Technician
- Neil Williams, Water Resource Engineer
- Richard Wiltshire, Geotechnical Engineer, USBR
- Gary Witt, Hydrogeologist

Finally, I must also dedicate this book to Ruth Wright, the energetic, intrepid, and talented photographer, historian, and organizer, who joined in all the research and helped to solve the many riddles with which we were faced.

1

Solving Mesa Verde Mysteries

PEOPLE OFTEN ASK how an attorney who served in the Colorado Legislature and an engineer (my wife and I) got started on research into ancient public works projects at Mesa Verde. It was easy! In fact, once we realized what could be learned using our knowledge and tools, there was no choice but to plunge in.

It was a beautiful Colorado morning in June 1995 when Ruth and I pulled up next to two energetic National Park Service archaeology rangers at the entrance to Mesa Verde National Park. That day rangers Cynthia Williams and Joel Brisbin were eager to take us to the anomalous Morefield Mound in Morefield Canyon, Far View Reservoir on Chapin Mesa, and a series of stone-walled terraces in a gully bottom that they called check dams. Unknown to Ruth and me, the rangers had a hidden agenda: they wanted to pique our interest in the potential study of these prehistoric public works structures.

Ruth and I had flown to nearby Durango, Colorado, to deliver a lecture to the Southwest Archaeological Society on one of our other research projects, the ancient Inca public works engineering at Machu Picchu in Peru. Our hosts had arranged the tour with the park rangers as a reward.

After entering Mesa Verde, we turned off the paved highway into Morefield Canyon on a fire access road. After we had passed through three sets of locked gates and driven down the canyon some 3 miles, Morefield Mound suddenly appeared (Figure 1.1). It was large and imposing, clearly outlined against the canyon wall behind it, which was covered in dark-green pine and juniper forest. Even though covered with thick sagebrush, it was obviously something special. On this first of our long series of pilgrimages to this lonely, enigmatic mound sitting on the wide canyon floor, a herd of wild horses grazing off in the distance watched us suspiciously.

Ruth and I walked over the mound and its berm to the north and tried to imagine what it could have been. Rangers Williams and Brisbin explained the contradictory opinions about the original purpose of the mound: a reservoir, a dance platform, or an erosional-terrace remnant of the Pleistocene era. Cynthia handed us a scholarly preliminary draft of a professional paper by Dr. Jack Smith, who had once served as chief archaeologist for

Figure 1.1: Morefield Reservoir sits on the valley floor with a flat top and a long berm that was the inlet canal. It has the appearance of a dance platform for ceremonies. (Ken Wright)

Mesa Verde National Park. Smith concluded that the mound had the sediment layering characteristics of a reservoir but that there was not a water supply to fill it. After looking at the canyon bottom, we thought Smith was right: there was no visible water supply. What could the mound have been?

Next our guides took us to a mysterious depression called Far View Reservoir on Chapin Mesa, where the Park Service had hedged its bets by erecting two interpretive signs. One said the mound had been a dance pavilion; the other said it had been a reservoir. But how would builders have filled the basin, and where was the water supply?

Ruth and I were drawn in. We spent the next eleven years studying reservoirs at Mesa Verde and have remained open to further potential studies on the horizon (Figure 1.2).

Why the Research?

Mesa Verde National Park has many mysteries that cry out for attention, but the four that interested us as water resource practitioners were the two described above and eventually another huge mound and a second large stone-walled depression.

Using science and engineering over an eleven-year period of field research and office analysis, we put to rest questions surrounding the

Figure 1.2: Ken Wright and Ruth Wright have studied ancient reservoirs at Mesa Verde since 1995. Ruth is shown with the Geoprobe used to drill into Box Elder Reservoir, our fourth project. (Ruth Wright and Gary Witt)

purpose of all four sites at Mesa Verde; there would be no more dis-agreement regarding their original functions. We were able to solve these problems because of cooperation and assistance from the National Park Service, financial help from the Colorado Historical Society, and advice and counsel from leading Southwestern archaeologists who helped us to ensure that our engineering findings fitted within the known scientific framework developed by Mesa Verde scholars.

We applied standard water resources and civil engineering method-ologies to the archaeological sites in a careful and patient manner; we fol-lowed the facts as they were defined. We call this process *paleohydrology:* the study of water use and water handling by ancient people. We began the nonprofit Wright Paleohydrological Institute in 1997 as an umbrella organization for our work at Machu Picchu; the umbrella was enlarged to encompass our work at Mesa Verde as well.

Applying paleohydrology became a driving force at Mesa Verde for several reasons: it provided a pathway to contribute to water-related knowledge about ancient civilizations and their capabilities, and it offered an opportunity to associate with seasoned archaeologists from whom we could learn much about focus, discipline, and documentation. Once we learned how well prehistoric people understood the engineering principles of hydrology and water harvesting, we felt compelled to tell their story so that others could more fully appreciate their skills at organization, planning, and building, and their dedication to the operation of public works. Little credit is given to the early Americans of the Southwest and Mesa Verde for their ability to build, maintain, and operate big projects in which organizational skills and technology transfer were essential. The engineers and scientists who joined our research team also benefited by working with archaeologists, seeing firsthand the fruits of the work of ancient engineers, and understanding that the study of ancient civilizations can contribute to making proper choices now to avoid repeating the mistakes of the past. Most of all, there was satisfaction in finding evidence of ancient thought processes and fingerprints on public works built more than one thousand years ago to serve their communities.

Mesa Verde and the Reservoirs

The evidence left behind by the Ancestral Puebloans of Mesa Verde (people sometimes referred to by archaeologists as the Anasazi) provides ample proof of civil engineering achievements that spanned hundreds of years (Figure 1.3). This field evidence rests in canyon bottoms and on mesa tops of Mesa Verde National Park, archaeological sites that were reservoirs for storage of domestic-use water. The four reservoirs we explored, analyzed, and documented are identified in Table 1.1.

Established by Congress in 1906, Mesa Verde National Park is an 81-square-mile national treasure in southwestern Colorado (Figures 1.4 and 1.5). In 1978 the United Nations designated the park as a World Heritage Site. In

Figure 1.3: Cliff-house dwellings of Mesa Verde demonstrate the ability of the Ancestral Puebloans to plan and build major projects. (Ken Wright)

Table 1.1 Mesa Verde Reservoirs			
Structure	Identification	Location	Time Span (A.D.)
Morefield	5MV1931	Morefield Canyon	750–100
Far View	5MV833	Chapin Mesa	950–1180
Sagebrush	5MV1936	unnamed mesa	950–1100
Box Elder	5MV4505	Prater Canyon	800–950

October 1999 the National Geographic Society ranked the park number six on its list of world wonders. In September 2004 the American Society of Civil Engineers (ASCE) designated the four reservoirs as a National Historic Civil Engineering Landmark, one of only 230 such landmarks in the world (Figure 1.6). The park is like a giant bank vault with upward of five thousand archaeological sites awaiting further study and interpretation (Figure 1.7). Usually only about three dozen sites are open to the public.

In 1995 we selected Morefield Reservoir in Morefield Canyon for intensive study (Figure 1.8). This site was our first enigma. What was a 16-foot-high mound doing on a rather flat, remote canyon bottom? The 220-foot-diameter mound had an upstream tail that, from the air, looked

Figure 1.4: Mesa Verde National Park is located in the high plateau country of the southwest corner of Colorado, about ten miles east of Cortez, Colorado, and about thirty-six miles west of Durango, Colorado. (Chris Brown)

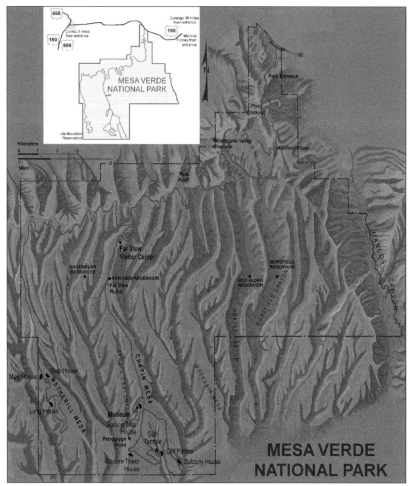

Figure 1.5: Mesa Verde National Park is a jewel of the National Park Service, a UN World Heritage Site, and a National Geographic Society World Wonder. Its 81 square miles contain prehistoric treasures that are yet to be studied and some that are yet to be discovered. This map shows the location of the four public works projects that are the subject of this book. (Wright Paleohydrological Institute)

like the handle of an inverted frying pan or even the tail of a fat pollywog, as shown in Figure 1.9. When our work started, one respected scientist thought the site had been a huge dance platform and that the upstream tail had been an approach walkway. Another scientist, from Arizona, said it was the erosional remnant of a prehistoric terrace. Dr. Jack Smith, who was chair of the University of Colorado–Denver Department of Anthropology and later served as chief archaeologist of the park, had concluded in

Figure 1.6: Archaeologist David Breternitz stands behind the plaque commemorating the designation in 2004 of the reservoirs at Mesa Verde as a National Historic Civil Engineering Landmark by the American Society of Civil Engineers. (Ruth Wright)

Figure 1.7: The Ancestral Puebloans left behind abundant evidence of their public works skills and civil engineering achievements at Far View Reservoir on Chapin Mesa of Mesa Verde National Park. In 1999 the National Park Service changed the name from Mummy Lake to Far View Reservoir because by then the site's original purpose and function had been proven by the 1998–1999 engineering studies. (National Park Service File)

a 1967 study that the site had all the signs of a prehistoric reservoir, minus an apparent water supply. This was the second enigma. According to Smith, "there just was not enough runoff." In light of these doubts, Smith did not publish his 1967 results until 1999, after engineering studies had provided the needed evidence that a water supply did in fact exist, and that the accumulated sediments and maize pollen in the mound could have been deposited there only by flowing water. By coupling engineering data with archaeological data, the mysteries of the Morefield Mound were systematically laid to rest.

Puebloan Hydraulics

Early Americans created viable and active settlements in the Mesa Verde area over a 750-year period, from about A.D. 550 to 1300 (Table 1.2). The public works research related to reservoirs has identified the period from A.D. 750 to 1180 with reservoir building and operation. Archaeologists have divided the 750-year time span into distinct periods for study purposes, with the Pueblo I and II periods best representing the time of the four Mesa Verde reservoirs.

The Ancestral Puebloans had no written language; they did not have bronze, iron, or steel; and they did not use the wheel, although they did

Figure 1.8: Excavation of Morefield Reservoir was conducted in 1997 by the paleohydrology team to determine the purpose and function of the large mound. The trench provided a detailed look at what happened there from A.D. 750 to 1100. (Ken Wright)

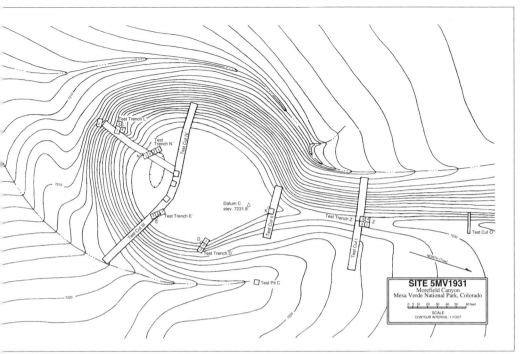

Figure 1.9: Morefield Reservoir, with its inlet canal to the right, has the shape of a huge pollywog or an inverted frying pan. Some thought it might be a dance platform with an approach walkway. This map was prepared by Dr. Jack Smith in 1967. (Jack Smith)

Table 1.2
Time Periods of Mesa Verde

Period	Time Span (A.D.)
Basketmaker III	550–750
Pueblo I	750–900
Pueblo II	900–1100
Pueblo III	1100–1300

use stone to good advantage (Figures 1.10 and 1.11). As a result, American history books tend to underrate them in terms of technical capabilities and social organization. However, as will be demonstrated, the Ancestral Puebloans had a rudimentary knowledge of hydrological phenomena, water transport, and storage. To build reservoirs, they also had good organizational capabilities; otherwise their large public works efforts requiring large-scale continuous operation and maintenance work would not have been possible.

Figure 1.10: A stone found near Sagebrush Reservoir showed Ancestral Puebloans' stoneworking abilities. The ax head is of porphyry, a material foreign to Mesa Verde National Park. (Ken Wright)

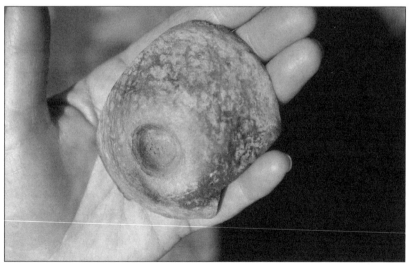

Figure 1.11: This palm stone was found at a pueblo near Box Elder Reservoir. It would have been used for fire making. (Ken Wright)

To create Morefield Reservoir, the Mesa Verdeans first excavated a pond on the valley bottom to reach the periodic shallow water table and to capture infrequent storm runoff. The stored runoff carried sediment that needed to be periodically dredged and cast to the side using crude tools. Because dredging did not remove all the sediment during each cleaning, it was not long before the pond bottom began to rise in elevation and take the form of a mound into which water would no longer flow by gravity. The Mesa Verdeans determined that water could be diverted from the canyon bottom into a delivery canal leading to the rising pond, but sediment deposits still had to be regularly cleaned out and cast to the side, forming berms. By A.D. 1100, this process had raised the Morefield Reservoir some 21 feet above the original pond bottom of 350 years earlier (Figure 1.12). Not only did the public works of the Mesa Verdeans have to withstand drainage-basin forest fires and floods, they were also subjected to a regular upstream relocation of their point of diversion. This was done to gain elevation advantage for gravity flow to the rising reservoir pool. Each time the point of diversion for the inlet canal was relocated, the Mesa Verdeans had to raise the canal elevation to keep up with the rising elevation of the water system. Eventually the canal was on an elevated berm, which created the tail portion of the tadpole image.

Study of two canyon-bottom reservoirs, Morefield and Box Elder (Figure 1.13) in Morefield and Prater Canyons, respectively, showed enough similarities to prove that technology transfer between the populations of these two canyons existed as early as about A.D. 800.

In the tenth century other Pueblo II people, living on mesa tops rather than in the canyon bottoms, constructed two additional reservoirs that modern engineers would have judged to be ill directed and doomed to failure. There was no natural drainage basin for either, and the natural soil surface had a high infiltration rate. The Ancestral Puebloans had learned, however, that the soil contained enough silt and clay particles that when the soil was puddled, the silt and clay migrated to the surface, creating a highly impervious surface. Nearby areas that were subjected to busy foot traffic, such as well-traveled paths, the environs of pueblos, and upslope agricultural fields, created runoff from even small rainfalls. Realizing that a half acre of such impervious surface could generate a substantial volume of runoff from only a half inch of intense rainfall, the Ancestral Puebloans began harvesting water. Interceptor ditches needed to route the limited runoff to their newly created depressions for storage resulted in Far View Reservoir (a.k.a. Mummy Lake) and Sagebrush Reservoir (Figures 1.14 and 1.15).

All four of the reservoirs have enough similarities, even though two are in canyon bottoms and two are on mesa tops, to identify the successful transfer of public works technology from canyon bottom to mesa top, from settlement to settlement, and from generation to generation.

Figure 1.12: The 1997 Morefield Reservoir excavation wall is carefully examined by team member John Rold, former state geologist. The team carefully studied all the evidence found in the trench wall along with the hydrology data and concluded that a water supply had existed. (Ruth Wright)

Figure 1.13: Box Elder Reservoir mound in Prater Canyon was covered with sagebrush until the Bircher Fire of 2000. The sagebrush effectively hid the reservoir until its chance discovery in September 2001. This view is looking east from Site 5MV3190. (Ken Wright)

Figure 1.14: The soils of sand, silt, and clay of Far View Reservoir were examined in detail through the use of hand augers. Here engineer Bastiaan Lammers conducts a probe of the soils near the early intake ditch. We found that the soils, when wetted and packed, tended to be impervious. (Ruth Wright)

Figure 1.15: The 1972–1974 trenches excavated into Sagebrush Reservoir are shown in the center of the aerial photo. The two trees just to the right of the horizontal trench grow on a pueblo archaeological site known as 5MV2036. A fire access road is shown at upper right. (Jack Smith)

2

Mesa Verde in a Nutshell

EARLY NATIVE AMERICANS knew about the wonders of southwestern Colorado when they, as foragers of the Archaic Period, camped there as early as 8,500 years ago. They knew the environment and climate would be conducive to a good lifestyle. These hardy people hunted small game; gathered fruits, nuts, and seeds; and made baskets for carrying, cooking, and storing. They used stone implements and tools but had no pottery and did not grow their food.

The Magical Plant

Perhaps five thousand to six thousand years ago, the people of Mexico found that they could grow and even improve a natural woody grass (teosinte) that grew in their highlands. By choosing the best seeds from year to year, they eventually produced what we call maize (corn)—a thoroughly domesticated species. By 1400 B.C., maize had reached both Mexican coasts, where it became a popular food staple contributing to stability and population growth.

About 1000 B.C., maize came to southwestern Colorado Native Americans (Figure 2.1). For some groups this magical plant provided an "insurance policy" when other food could not be found. Others found the new food source so significant that they settled down to tend their fields instead of moving from camp to camp.

The maize pollen found in the sediments of all four Mesa Verde reservoirs that we studied from 1995 to 2004 demonstrated that the seeds of this magical plant thrived in the good soils, even with the limited water supply. Technology transfer from Mexico changed the way people lived and allowed them to thrive.

Basketmaker II

Table 2.1 summarizes ancient settlement of Mesa Verde in southwestern Colorado, beginning with the Basketmaker II population. The Basketmaker II people were early Colorado residents for 1,500 years, from 1000 B.C. to A.D. 500, and are known for their agriculture, atlatl spear-thrower, and sophisticated baskets (Figures 2.2 and 2.3). It is known from field evidence

15

Figure 2.1: The advent of corn production allowed the Ancestral Puebloans to increase their calorie intake and begin to focus on building communities and harvesting water. This illustration is of an ear of corn found in a Basketmaker cave. (Sally Kribs)

that the Durango area was favored by these first Colorado settlers at Talus Village and at the North and South Falls Creek Shelters as early as 322 B.C., but they also spread out farther to places that suited them, such as Tamarron, north of Durango; the Pine River valley near Ignacio, Colorado; and sites in the Dolores River basin where soil, water, and sunshine provided what they needed.

The Basketmaker II people relied on their maize, supplementing it with squash, piñon nuts, grass seeds, deer, rabbit, and even bighorn sheep. Wild turkey was a delicacy. For some unexplained reason, the early Americans, prior to A.D. 550, avoided Mesa Verde. Perhaps there just were not enough people to go around. The settlement of Mesa Verde would be left to later generations, even though, for hunting and gathering, groups would have routinely ventured into its canyons and onto its mesas.

Basketmaker III

In about A.D. 550 the descendants of the Basketmaker II people discovered the significance of the fertile soils of Mesa Verde; we know these people as Basketmaker III. Some of the families who homesteaded on Mesa Verde at that time abandoned the reliable flowing waters of the Animas and La Plata Rivers for the lush, forested mesas and deep canyons of Mesa Verde, where the canyons seldom carried surface-water flow. They numbered at most a few hundred people. Numerous other communities of scattered Basketmaker III farmsteads sprang up elsewhere in southwestern Colorado, wherever there were good soils, streams, and relatively adequate rainfall. They were lucky; between A.D. 570 and 700, southwestern Colorado had decent climate conditions, and this new area took on a decided agricultural character. Their homes—pit houses—were half dug into the soil and half above ground (Figures 2.4 and 2.5). By the end of the period,

Table 2.1
Ancient Inhabitants of Southwest U.S.

Group	Era	Settlement Locations	Characteristics
Basketmaker II	1000 B.C.–A.D. 500	Talus Village Falls Creek Tamarron Pine River Valley Dolores River Basin Canyon De Chelly	Sturdy mud homes Sophisticated baskets Agriculture • maize • squash • piñon nuts • grass seeds Atlatl spear-thrower
Basketmaker III	A.D. 500–750	Mesa Verde Southern Utah Hovenweep Northeastern Arizona	Pit houses Agriculture • bean added to diet Pottery-making began Bow and arrow
Pueblo I	A.D. 750–900	Mesa Verde Chaco Canyon Hovenweep Northeastern Arizona	Surface homes More complex pottery
Pueblo II	A.D. 900–1100	Mesa Verde Hovenweep Chaco Canyon Jemez Mountains Bandelier Montezuma Valley Northeastern Arizona	Stone masonry began Agriculture • softer corn developed More sophisticated arrowheads
Pueblo III	A.D. 1100–1300	Movement from Mesa Verde canyons and mesa tops to cliff dwellings about A.D. 1200 Then, about A.D. 1250, movement from Mesa Verde to Little Colorado and Rio Grande River basins In Arizona and New Mexico Canyon De Chelly Northeastern Arizona	Large villages Very sophisticated pottery

Figure 2.2: The atlatl spear-thrower has finger loops that hold a dart or spear in a groove and project it at high velocity. The atlatl provided greater range than a thrown spear but was eventually replaced by the bow and arrow. (Sally Kribs)

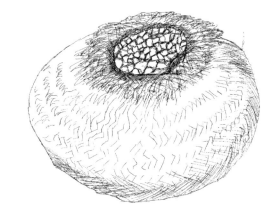

Figure 2.3: A typical yucca Basketmaker basket with corn. (Sally Kribs)

southwestern Colorado was the home of many villages and several thousand occupants. Though not a lot by modern standards, this growth heralded a real population expansion of prehistoric people in permanent communities tending to agriculture, firing pottery, and adopting the use of the bow and arrow. Historians think of the sixth century as the time when Colorado was first settled. With 130 years of somewhat reliable rainfall, a way of life that remains based on agriculture to this day was begun.

Mesa Verde was a good choice for settling down. It had loess, a wind-blown deposit of 3 feet of soil that had blown in from Monument Valley about fifteen thousand years earlier. In the sixth century Mesa Verde was a fertile place for growing crops. Thick forests of pine and juniper provided privacy, security, isolation, building materials, and fuel. Sunshine warmed the south-facing canyons and tablelands. The people adapted so well that they and their descendants stayed for 750 years.

Pueblo I

There was a population expansion by A.D. 750. By this time the resident population of southwestern Colorado was well over three thousand for the first time in prehistory, and the people's pottery-making skills had improved. We call them Pueblo I people.

Figure 2.4: A Basketmaker III pit house was half in the ground and half aboveground. It was entered through the roof. These early Americans made good use of structural poles. (Ken Wright)

Figure 2.5: One of the few good places to see Basketmaker III pit houses next to a much later Pueblo III ruin is Step House, where six hundred years separate the phases of construction. (Ken Wright)

For the Pueblo I community in Mesa Verde, the biggest challenge was the relative aridity—an average of 18 inches of rainfall per year, with 13 to 15 inches at lower elevations between about 6,000 and 7,000 feet. These settlers had to dig deep into their creativity, leadership skills, and community spirit to survive, even flourish, in spite of the dearth of water. Their dry-land farming atop mesas and in canyons relied on limited groundwater, snowmelt, and occasional summer rains. But maize, the magical plant, was adaptable to a wide variety of environmental conditions. Crop failure was common, but they persisted. They started building rooms aboveground, while their pit houses were transitioning into kivas (Figures 2.6 and 2.7). This allowed a larger grouping of people into communities with a semblance of social order and the related benefits. During the cold, hard winters, they retreated into their pit houses and kivas to exploit the earth's warmth and avoid exposure to howling winds and plunging temperatures. Over the next century the Mesa Verde population increased to about one thousand. Housing improvements and kivas made life somewhat easier, but the relative scarcity of water remained a problem. Community life meant that amenities could now be developed that were impossible for small, isolated groups.

These Pueblo I people clearly knew how to excavate. A great kiva they built in Morefield Canyon between 829 and 865, and left almost intact for modern scientists to study, measures 55 feet in diameter and 7 feet

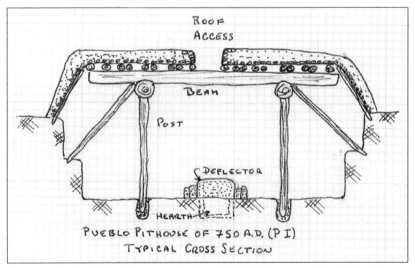

Figure 2.6: The Pueblo I pit house was built partially into the ground to gain heat from the soil and to provide protection against cold winters. (Ken Wright)

Figure 2.7: By about A.D. 900, the construction of kivas, a natural evolution from the pit houses, was well established. (Ruth Wright)

deep (Figure 2.8). It is carefully designed and constructed and must have made a fine place for religious rituals, meetings, and winter shelter. It is an extraordinary example of the work and effort of many people striving toward a community goal. We can surmise that these prodigious diggers also burrowed into the canyons' alluvium to unearth groundwater. A hole filled with fresh, clean water, especially in springtime when the water table was high, would have been a blessing.

After our 1995–1997 excavations and paleohydrological analyses, we proved that a mound in Morefield Canyon was actually a reservoir. When we analyzed and dated the reservoir, we realized that its commencement predated the great kiva by eighty years, indicating that the first priority had been a water supply. After the water supply was secured, the people could use their organizational and building skills to create a more developed and well-rounded society. They dug a shallow pond in Morefield Canyon about A.D. 750, squarely in the canyon's normally dry bottom, the thalweg ("valley way"). The land cover had changed over the years because of forest fires, considerable clearing of timber for building and fuel, and the planting of maize in the upper part of the valley. The result of these changes was that the earth absorbed much less water, and now there was more runoff than in earlier days. This was just fine for filling their pond,

Figure 2.8: The Morefield Canyon Great Kiva, just downstream from Morefield Reservoir, was excavated in 1965 by Jack Smith under the direction of Robert Lister. It was built about A.D. 860 during the Pueblo I period. (Jack Smith)

even though erosion had increased. These and similar technological developments led to an overall southwestern Colorado population increase to about nine thousand by the mid-850s.

The rains that came, especially late-summer rains from the monsoon phenomenon, now occasionally flowed down the thalweg, filling the pond. This flow also brought the silt and sand from hillside erosion into the water hole, which the people dredged using sticks, antlers, stones, and baskets. These dredged sediments eventually formed a berm. Dredging took a lot of organization and energy but was necessary for maintaining this water resource. Pretty soon the rising bottom meant that water would no longer flow into the pond. Rather than digging another pond, the early settlers built an inlet canal to bring in water by gravity flow. Addressing and finding a solution to this hydraulic challenge required creativity, leadership, and organized community effort.

The success of the technology of the Morefield Canyon people inspired their "cousins" in Prater Canyon immediately to the west. The Prater Canyon Reservoir was started in A.D. 800, using precisely the same technology, and was built on an exact east-west line from the neighbors' public works project. The Prater Canyon community grew to about three hundred residents who enjoyed the land, water, and sunshine of the west slope of the canyon bottom. Our palynology studies showed that maize agriculture was extensive. We found large amounts of maize pollen in all the layers of Box Elder Reservoir.

The Pueblo I Coloradoans of the ninth century were industrious, as shown by the field evidence that we found. An antler excavated from Morefield Reservoir, carbon dated to A.D. 860, showed that dredging of the sediments occurred at the same time that the community was in the middle of the massive construction project for the great kiva that is designated 5MV3130. They had enough people to grow maize, cut timber, and support the reservoir and kiva workers. Someone had to organize all the effort and make sure that everyone contributed to the community's well-being.

Pueblo II

Around A.D. 900, with drier weather, the Mesa Verde area population seems to have decreased. We do not know why, but emigration likely played a part. The whole Southwest had a population decline at this time, but Mesa Verde, because of its good location, soils, and rainfall, seems to have been hit less hard than other parts of the region. We know this because the operation of Morefield Reservoir and the reservoir in the adjacent Prater Canyon, Box Elder Reservoir, continued without interruption. Pottery became more sophisticated (Figure 2.9), periodic water shortages were still the norm, and the people evolved into what we know as the Pueblo II culture. Village layouts became more refined (Figure 2.10). Even with fewer people, the communities kept operating and maintaining the reservoirs as their predecessors had done. By about A.D. 950 Morefield Reservoir stood 21 feet higher than the water hole of 150 years before, and the inlet canal had been extended upstream in the canyon to reach the higher elevation required to fill the reservoir by gravity.

By A.D. 950 Box Elder Reservoir had been in use 150 years, and it had risen 20 feet from its original elevation. Apparently it became too costly in effort and manpower to maintain, and the residents ceased to store water there. However, they continued an active and thriving occupation of the canyon bottom, with frequent visits to Morefield Canyon, where they would enjoy the great kivas (of which there were now two) and perhaps

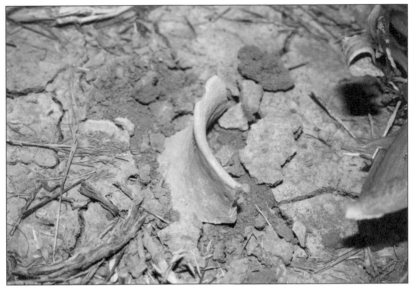

Figure 2.9: This fragment of a jar for carrying water was found at Morefield Reservoir in 1997. (Gary Witt)

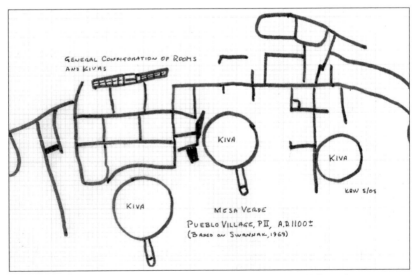

Figure 2.10: The Pueblo II villages (A.D. 900–1100) had evolved to buildings above ground, but with deep kivas for social gatherings and warmth during the cold winters. (Ken Wright)

collect a few jars of water. An ancient foot trail still goes up and over the ridge between Prater Canyon and Morefield Canyon, and we were able to hike from Box Elder Reservoir to the great kiva in only an hour. Due to the close proximity, good land, some water, and an amenable environment, it is probable that the Morefield community expanded up and over the mesa to incorporate with the Prater Canyon valley bottom.

Meanwhile, also in A.D. 950, mesa-top pueblo "relatives," some 4 miles away on Chapin Mesa and on another mesa 1 mile west of Chapin, noted the success of Morefield Reservoir and decided to build domestic storage ponds of their own, but on mesa tops rather than in canyon bottoms. These reservoirs are called Far View and Sagebrush Reservoirs, respectively. Modern engineers would not have attempted the construction of these reservoirs because there simply was no water supply to be stored. Yet they did work. We know this because our field investigations showed that the silt and sand left in the two mesa-top reservoirs were waterborne, carried in by ditches that intercepted water harvested from packed-down areas. The Puebloans knew more about the hydrology of mesa runoff than modern engineers and had learned that silt and clay particles, when packed by bare feet and sandals and puddled with rainfall, would float up to form an impervious surface. The soil surface would then become as tight as a parking lot with nearly 100 percent runoff. Even a small area of half an acre could be successful for water harvesting.

Times became more and more difficult for the Ancestral Puebloans. Forests thinned by fires, lumber harvesting, and erosion lowered the water tables in the canyons. However, the isolation of Mesa Verde meant it still provided a good place to live, farm, and survive. A healthy individual who survived childhood stresses might be able to live as long as fifty to fifty-five years, about the same life span as that of Europeans at the time, or perhaps even a little longer. This meant that the Pueblo II people increased in population, perhaps limited only by the carrying capacity of their neighborhoods.

Pueblo III

By A.D. 1100 another transition began to occur. Morefield and Sagebrush Reservoirs had been abandoned. The Mesa Verde population had increased to about 1,500. Pottery evolved to styles named Mesa Verde Corrugated and Mancos Black on White (Figure 2.11). Mesa Verde residents moved into a new phase that we call Pueblo III. The nearby timber was being depleted, and the increased runoff had gullied the lush valley bottoms, resulting in less groundwater being readily available. Intense use of Chapin Mesa, for instance, had resulted in deforestation and soil erosion. Disease played a part in the survival effort of the population, and life was less certain.

Regional changes happened too. Shortly after A.D. 1100, the Chaco Canyon system in New Mexico declined and came to an end; a population center to the north named Aztec had been started with a few large construction efforts there around A.D. 1110 to 1120. Then it became so dry that well-planned, Chacoan-style building projects that involved bringing a large quantity of timber from distant mountains had ceased by 1135 or 1140. It was then that Chaco area-wide control diminished and the social order began to disintegrate, leading to a degree of civil unrest. The dryness lasted for about fifty years, and the drought was so bad that even the area that is now the central United States felt it. The land experienced a kind of desertification. Sand began blowing in northeastern Colorado, and dunes formed along the South Platte River near modern-day Hillrose. The hardy people of Mesa Verde withstood the drought for some years, but by A.D. 1180 even Far View Reservoir had been abandoned as a domestic water supply. It no longer worked well as a reservoir, although the stone enclosure

Figure 2.11: Mancos Black-on-White pottery. These bowl rims were found at Morefield Reservoir. (Ken Wright)

was likely used as a gathering place for various purposes. Its ceremonial-quality stairway served more than just an ordinary utilitarian function for water collection. The people of Far View Village, Pipe Shrine House, and Coyote Village now had to trek down into the canyon to gather water.

During the late twelfth century mesa tops and canyon bottoms ceased being the best places to live. The people began moving into large cliff over-hangs, where they transferred their public works building technology to cliff houses while still farming on the mesa tops (Figure 2.12). Cliff houses provided good defensive positions against marauding strangers, and there were plenty of cliff recesses that caught the winter sunshine that brought warmth. Cliff Palace, Spruce Tree House, Balcony House, and many other cliff dwellings took shape. Construction methods were good; the people planned to stay a long time, even though they did not actually do so. Lots of kivas would provide spaces for community meetings, religious cere-monies, and warmer rooms in the winter. Both Cliff Palace and Spruce Tree House had springs. In some places several cliff dwellings centered on one good spring. Other cliff houses did their best with canyon-bottom excavations to the water table and the use of small seeps.

Figure 2.12: The cliff dwellings at Mesa Verde are popular attractions for tourists of all ages. They inspire awe because they are akin to modern apartment houses. (Ruth Wright)

After nearly another one hundred years, the drought of A.D. 1275 hit Mesa Verde hard, but by this time some families had already left for places to the south. The population was dropping. The last timber, according to David Breternitz, was placed at Cliff Palace in A.D. 1287. Life at Mesa Verde had become too uncertain, and besides, a better lifestyle along the Rio Grande River, in locations such as Casas Grande in Arizona and even Paquime in old Mexico, beckoned, along with religious attractions. By A.D. 1300 the people had left in family and village groups, and Mesa Verde, their home for nearly eight hundred years, was deserted.

We know that the inhabitants of Mesa Verde and other southwestern Colorado communities did not just disappear; they moved on. From 1250 to 1300 population increased in the northern Rio Grande area, near what is now Santa Fe and Albuquerque, at the same time as the abandonment of southwestern Colorado. People in growing New Mexico communities were making pottery similar to the Pueblo III Mesa Verde styles. The people living there today have an oral tradition indicating that their ancestors migrated from the Mesa Verde region.

Studies at the Pinnacle archaeological site well south of Albuquerque show remarkable similarities to Mesa Verde area culture about 1300. This is likely one of the places that the early Colorado residents went. Here the immigrants found a good defensible rock outcrop, plenty of water, and tillable land that could be irrigated. Southwestern Colorado was now void of settlements; only foragers and transients were left to enjoy the valleys, streams, mesas, and forest environment until new people arrived.

3

Science and Engineering at Mesa Verde

MODERN SCIENTISTS AND ARCHAEOLOGISTS owe a great debt to the original explorers of Mesa Verde. Don Juan Maria de Rivera led what was likely the first expedition into the area in 1765. The first specific written mention of Mesa Verde comes from a geological report of the area by Professor J. S. Newberry in 1859. In 1874 William Henry Jackson photographed the Two Story Cliff House and other Mesa Verde attractions. Other notable explorers of Mesa Verde include the Wetherill brothers, Richard, Al, John, and Clayton; W. H. Holmes; S. E. Osborn; Charles Mason; and Baron Gustaf E. A. Nordenskiold, all of whom worked in the park before 1900.

Two of the four Mesa Verde reservoirs that we studied have long been the subject of scholarly interest and discourse, Far View Reservoir since 1892 and Morefield Reservoir since 1914. The other two, Sagebrush and Box Elder, lay hidden under sagebrush until 1964 and 2001, respectively. Table 3.1 summarizes the notable researchers who studied these Mesa Verde reservoirs.

Past Reservoir Research

In 1892, in a narrative of an expedition to Mesa Verde, explorer Frederick H. Chapin estimated that cliff dwellings might have housed four hundred to five hundred people on Chapin Mesa (Figure 3.1) near Far View Reservoir. Chapin was the first scientist known to have described the site as a water storage facility. In 1917 Smithsonian scientist Jesse W. Fewkes also identified the site as a lake (Figure 3.2). In 1934 the renowned Southwestern archaeologist Earl Morris excavated a test pit at the site in an unsuccessful search for features associated with great kivas. In 1950 James A. Lancaster exposed what he thought to be a west-side intake ditch, a revetment (an embankment), and a long canal leading from the lake for irrigation. The Morris and Lancaster studies, although scientifically valuable, provided no definitive information. Art Rohn later studied Chapin Mesa in detail. What had appeared to be a prehistoric irrigation ditch was actually an old road.

Late-twentieth-century investigations mostly broke with the reservoir theory, especially in 1986, when hydrological modeling confirmed that Far View Reservoir was far from any known water supply. But David Breternitz

Table 3.1	
Summary of Researchers at Mesa Verde Reservoirs	
Representative Year	Researcher
Far View Reservoir	
1892	Frederick H. Chapin
1917	Jesse W. Fewkes
1934	Earl Morris
1950	James "Al" Lancaster
1969	David Breternitz
	Art Rohn
1998	WPI* and WWE**
Morefield Reservoir	
1929	Harold S. Gladwin
1960	Wetherill Mesa Archaeological Project
1962	Richard Woodbury
	Arthur Rohn
1965	Robert H. Lister
1967	Jack Smith
	Ezra Zubrow
1995	WPI and WWE
Sagebrush Reservoir	
1964	Alden Hayes
1967	George McLellan
1972	Jack Smith
2000	WPI and WWE
Box Elder Reservoir	
2001	James Kleidon
2002	WPI and WWE
* Wright Paleohydrological Institute	
** Wright Water Engineers, Inc.	

of the University of Colorado (Figure 3.3) held to the reservoir theory. Having excavated the site in 1969, Breternitz belatedly published his findings in 1999. He stood by five conclusions:

1. Around A.D. 950–1000, the Ancestral Puebloans built Far View Reservoir to exploit Chapin Mesa's sparse surface runoff.
2. Far View Reservoir was periodically desilted and remodeled in an attempt to make it more effective, and probably in response to changing climatic and cultural factors.
3. Far View Reservoir ceased to be utilized in the latter half of the 1100s, at the same time that the sixteen habitation sites in the Far View group were abandoned.

Figure 3.1: This early Mesa Verde photograph dated around 1916 shows a pack train stopping at a dry Far View Reservoir. Far View Village lies about 1000 feet to the right. Even in those days, tourists flocked to Mesa Verde to view the cliff dwellings. (National Park Service File)

Figure 3.2: The ethnologist for the Smithsonian Institution, Dr. Jesse Walter Fewkes (1850–1930) (center), directed the excavation of Far View Village in 1916. Prior to the excavation, Far View Ruin appeared as a huge rubble mound with trees and bushes growing on it. Notice the team of mules hooked to a sledge for moving rock rubble. (National Park Service File)

Figure 3.3: Dr. David Breternitz is a scholarly researcher who is happiest in the field and in the excavations. His publication on Mesa Verde ceramics is the industry standard. (Ruth Wright)

4. Far View Reservoir was never a reliable or more than a seasonal source of domestic water for the nearby habitation sites.
5. Although the Ancestral Puebloans devoted tremendous effort to harvesting their most precious commodity, water, the system was probably both inefficient and unreliable.

Morefield Reservoir made its first appearance in a scientific publication as an archaeological feature on a 1914 U.S. Geological Survey (USGS) map. Harold S. Gladwin, who led a 1929 pottery-collecting expedition, erroneously described Morefield as "a dam site with a row of stones along the crest which appears to be part of the dam." Gladwin noted that potsherds were "scattered sparsely along the mound" and that the site "does not give the impression of having been houses."

In September 1960 several members of the Wetherill Mesa Archaeological Project visited Morefield Reservoir and reported "a feature which suggested the possibility of having once been a storage tank for runoff water from the talus slopes and the mesa forming the east wall of [Morefield] canyon." The archaeological project took a particular interest in possible evidence for the catching and storing of runoff for domestic purposes. Team members wondered if the site in Morefield Canyon might help explain water supply elsewhere on the mesa. Two years later archaeologist Richard Woodbury, assisted by Arthur Rohn of the Wetherill Mesa Archaeological Project, collected potsherds and stone artifacts specifically related to water management. Rohn continued the work during 1963. The investigations produced a topographic map confirming that the intake berm stood high enough to conduct water into the reservoir. Later Orville Parsons of the U.S. Department of Agriculture collected two long core samples from the sediments of Morefield Reservoir and concluded that there was evidence of possible irrigation in Morefield Canyon. Rohn, Woodbury, Parsons, and Jack Smith felt that this reservoir had provided domestic water, not irrigation water. In 1997, based on detailed inspections and evaluations of Morefield Canyon hydrology and field evidence, team members Wright and Smith determined that there had been no irrigation other than that which could be attributed to a seasonal high-water table.

In 1965 Robert H. Lister of the University of Colorado began archaeological studies in Morefield Canyon, where he excavated two great kivas, a Pueblo I village, a small hilltop kiva, and a village site. In 1967 he assigned Smith and then graduate student Ezra Zubrow to excavate the Morefield Mound (Figure 3.4). Although Smith and Zubrow's thorough and

Figure 3.4: In 1967 Ezra Zubrow (left) and Ted Weber (right) assisted Dr. Jack Smith in the early scientific studies of the Morefield Mound in Morefield Canyon. They could not prove that the mound had been a reservoir. (National Park Service File)

scholarly handling of the excavation and analysis was not published for twenty-two years, their findings provided the foundation for the 1995–1997 paleohydrological study of Morefield Reservoir.

The third reservoir site appeared in literature in 1964 when Alden Hayes visited the site that we now know as Sagebrush Reservoir. In 1967 George McLellan of the University of Colorado excavated at Sagebrush Reservoir to determine whether it had been a great kiva, but his work was never completed. Then, in 1972 and 1974, Smith performed extensive excavation at the site and prepared detailed profiles and cross-sections coupled with the scientific collection of pottery shards and soil samples (Figure 3.5). Smith's work provided an excellent starting point for paleohydrological studies at Sagebrush Reservoir in 2000 and 2001; however, he would not define the site as a reservoir because of the apparent total lack of any natural drainage basin or water supply.

Meanwhile, the fourth reservoir, which we know as Box Elder Reservoir, was not discovered until 2001, following the 2000 Bircher Forest Fire (Figure 3.6). National Park Service archaeologist James Kleidon initially documented it in September 2001, when he identified it as a Pueblo I reservoir on the basis of surface pottery artifacts and a shape similar to that of Morefield Reservoir. In 2002 Kleidon's appraisal was judged by me to be correct.

Figure 3.5: Much is owed to the Mesa Verde archaeologists who have studied and interpreted the field evidence. Here, Dr. Jack Smith carefully draws trench details at Sagebrush Reservoir in 1974. (National Park Service File)

Figure 3.6: The fourth reservoir studied by the paleohydrology team was Box Elder Reservoir, seen here from the east. The light-colored slopes are the reservoir sides, with the water storage area represented by the darker vegetation. The forest devastation due to the 2000 Bircher Fire is apparent both in the foreground and background. (Ken Wright)

From 1969 to 1995 there were no significant water reservoir field research projects conducted at the national park other than those by Smith and by Timothy Weston, who reported on a site on Park Mesa. In 1995 I was invited by Ranger Cynthia Williams to examine the Morefield Mound and the Far View Reservoir archaeological sites for possible water research study. Williams encouraged me to seek a national park research permit, and my company Wright Water Engineers, Inc., of Denver, Colorado, commenced fieldwork in October 1995. The Colorado Historical Society provided financial support for the public works engineering study. The 1995–1997 field research at Morefield Reservoir was followed by similar work at Far View Reservoir from 1998 to 1999, at Sagebrush Reservoir from 2000 to 2001, and finally at Box Elder Reservoir from 2002 to 2003.

The Paleohydrological Investigation

Webster's Third International Dictionary defines paleohydrology as "the study of ancient use and handling of water." Our research at Mesa Verde was aimed at that definition. Designed to be easily implemented and effective, it had to fit within the strict field protocol the National Park

Service has developed to protect this treasure house of archaeological sites. Fortunately, we had the assistance of park archaeological professionals Linda Towle, Larry Nordby, and Cynthia Williams. Chief Ranger Charlie Peterson assisted as well. After the initial field study exploration trip, Jack Smith, former chief archaeologist of the national park, joined the research team as scientific adviser. Smith was instrumental in ensuring that engineering and hydrologic findings were interpreted in a manner consistent with Mesa Verde's long history of scientific research.

Many specialists on our research team provided the breadth of experience to conduct a wide variety of technical investigations. The analyses typically applied at each reservoir site included procedures that, when integrated, would elucidate the purpose and function of each site and provide evidence as to how the site was developed, how and when it was used and the likely characteristics of operation and maintenance.

- *Field topographic surveys* used traditional civil engineering technology such as theodolites, level instruments, measuring tapes, and plane tables. We defined and mapped the topography so that shapes of features, heights of mounds, and lengths of canal routes could be calculated. Field surveying was critical to the paleohydrological studies (Figure 3.7).

Figure 3.7: Field topographic surveys were important to the paleohydrology studies. Here, hydrologist Chris Crowley operates his theodolite in the center of Far View Reservoir. (Ruth Wright)

- *Soil augering* was done to recover soil profile data from the archaeological sites and so that sediment layering could be specifically defined, along with charcoal evidence. In natural soil areas, we confirmed the character of the soils (Figure 3.8).

- *Surface infiltration tests* provided site-specific data on present-day infiltration rates of bare and vegetated soils with an indication of typical permeability. This data provided for estimates of rainfall-runoff relationships (Figure 3.9).

- *Geologic descriptions* were necessary so that there would be an understanding of the basin characteristics and the source of eroded materials. We needed to define bedrock outcrops and faults (Figure 3.10).

- *Geomorphological analyses* provided information on the character of valley bottoms that allowed an evaluation of likely prehistoric canyon-bottom conditions encountered by the Mesa Verdeans (Figure 3.11).

- *Ceramic analysis* was important for estimating the period of human activity and reservoir dating. Much can be learned from the scientific study of pottery.

- *Paleo climate evaluations* using dendrochronology (tree rings) provided estimates of precipitation and temperature during prehistoric

Figure 3.8: Soil augers were used to penetrate the subsoil to collect samples for gradation analysis, soil character analysis, and pollen testing. (Ruth Wright)

Figure 3.9: The water runoff character of the surface soils was measured in the field using a standard infiltration ring. Lisa Klapper fills the ring prior to the actual test run. (Ruth Wright)

Figure 3.10: Hydrogeologist Eric Bikis (right) used geologic mapping to determine the characteristics of Sagebrush Reservoir with (left to right) Ken Wright, Ernest Pemberton, and David Breternitz. (Ruth Wright)

Figure 3.11: To determine the likely physical conditions of the canyon bottoms during prehistoric times, geomorphological studies were conducted and channel-bottom types documented. Ernest Pemberton, former chief sedimentation engineer for the Bureau of Reclamation, takes careful notes for his geomorphological analyses. (Ruth Wright)

times that related directly to water development needs and opportunities (Figure 3.12).

- *Rainfall-runoff determinations* were necessary to verify that the ancient structures were in fact water storage facilities and that a surface water supply actually existed.

- *Pollen analyses of prehistoric vegetation* provided important paleohydrological parameters so that the type and location of agricultural practices and the presence or absence of wetland plants could be determined. We defined forest successional periods and the presence or absence of sagebrush and medicinal plants.

- *Laboratory analyses of reservoir sediments* were done using hydrometer and sieve analyses of soils and sediments to define sand, silt, and clay content so that we could estimate sediment transport and depositional character.

- *A carbon-14 test* provided dating of Morefield Reservoir to supplement pottery analyses.

- *Groundwater evaluations* were useful in estimating available water sources and whether reservoir inflow might have originated via aquifers (Figure 3.13).

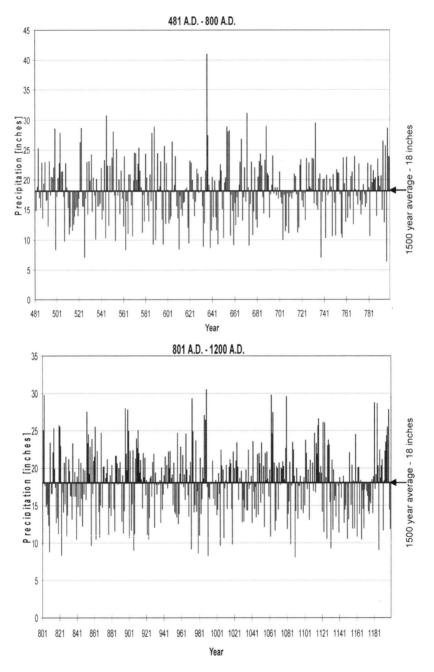

Figure 3.12: This estimate, by Dr. Jeffrey Dean, of Mesa Verde precipitation from A.D. 481 to 1988, was helpful in analyzing prehistoric precipitation at the four Mesa Verde reservoirs. (Source: Dr. Jeffrey Dean, Laboratory of Tree Ring Research)

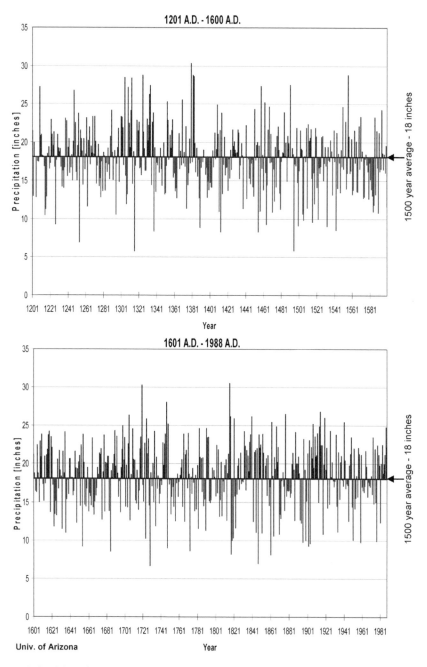

Periods of drought are illustrated by the accumulation of lines below the average line, representing years with a precipitation deficit. (Wright Paleohydrological Institute)

- *Archaeological studies* of the reservoir structures, canals, watersheds, and adjacent villages were necessary to allow the engineering data and studies to be properly placed in their anthropologic context and to provide a sound basis for their interpretation (Figure 3.14).
- *Aerial photos,* standard black-and-white, color, and infrared, were important in defining the ground conditions, identifying wetlands and water tables, and evaluating geomorphological processes (Figure 3.15).

Figure 3.13: Groundwater was an important component of the available prehistoric water supply. Members of the team test for depth to the water table in Morefield Canyon. (Ruth Wright)

Figure 3.14: Former Colorado state geologist John Rold examines Pueblo I and II village sites near Morefield Canyon. The rock shattered during the 2000 Bircher Fire. Forest fires cause great damage to archaeological sites. (Ruth Wright)

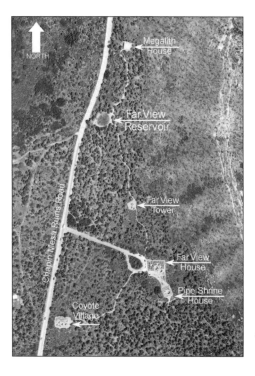

Figure 3.15: This aerial photograph of Chapin Mesa shows the relationship of Far View Reservoir to nearby ancient villages. (Wright Paleohydrological Institute)

4

Morefield Reservoir

Our study of the Morefield mound began in October 1995. Even at a controversial archaeological site in a sensitive, closed-off canyon of Mesa Verde National Park, we applied the common, modern methods of our engineering consulting practice. At first we were at a disadvantage because we had not yet met Dr. Jack Smith, formerly of the University of Colorado, the "guru" of Mesa Verde, who had served as chief archaeologist there for thirteen years. On all of our subsequent trips, Smith was an integral member of our research team. On the other hand, Ranger Archaeologist Cynthia Williams was with us to provide assurances as we tackled the initial fieldwork of surveying, mapping, and searching for clues. It was Ranger Williams who told us of Jack Smith and his long-ago draft paper on his work at the Morefield mound.

The first day was spent running a level survey loop from a downvalley USGS benchmark to the mound, examining the surrounding canyon bottom for ancient clues (there were many to the trained eye), and surveying cross-sections across the valley bottom and over the mound.

We worked hard the second day, even though a cold, wet, and windy snowfall started in midmorning. Thanks to warnings by Ranger Williams about how slippery the clay roadway would get with the wet snow, we left our research site in time and did not have to radio to Chief Ranger Charlie Peterson for assistance in driving out of the canyon.

What we learned from the first field trip into Morefield Canyon was that this enigmatic mound was no ordinary hill. To us this mound represented a wonderful opportunity to explore, test, study, and define a structure left by prehistoric people; it would be our job to help tell their remarkable story so that modern people would better understand them. We came away feeling that the facts would lead us to the right answer. Was it a ceremonial dance platform, an erosional remnant of a Pleistocene terrace, or a reservoir? We knew that much work lay ahead.

Densely populated by the tenth century A.D., Morefield Canyon contains the remains of two great kivas adjacent to villages. One kiva dates from the Pueblo I period (A.D. 750–900), the other from Pueblo II (A.D. 900–1100). The Ancestral Puebloans began Morefield Reservoir about a quarter-mile up the valley to the north, directly in the valley bottom (Figure 4.1). Today it resembles a huge dance platform mound with a flat top, complete with a berm that extends north, beginning at the same elevation as the top of the platform (Figure 4.2). It could have served as a good ceremonial structure. We now know, however, that the mound was once a reservoir fed by a canal that ran along the top of the berm.

The reservoir mound has a diameter of 220 feet at its base, with side slopes of 3:1 (horizontal:vertical) that rise up 16 feet to the flat top of the

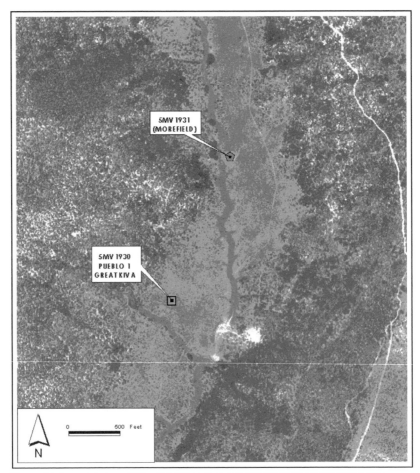

Figure 4.1: An aerial view of Morefield Canyon shows Morefield Reservoir about one-quarter mile north of a spectacular great kiva dating from the Pueblo I period. Adjacent to the kiva are many pueblo sites that represent the area of the highest density of former occupation in Mesa Verde National Park. The reservoir was originally begun in the channel of Morefield Canyon that now flows to its west. (Wright Paleohydrological Institute)

Figure 4.2: The huge mound of Morefield Reservoir sits on the floor of Morefield Canyon. It was formed by the inflow of sediments that were dredged from time to time to keep the reservoir operational. In over 350 years of operation (A.D. 750 – 1100), it rose 21 feet above its original bottom. (Ruth Wright)

mound, which is 130 feet in diameter (Figure 4.3) and shaped like a truncated cone. The mound is made up of layers of water-deposited sediment; sandy layers are interspersed with dense clay-silt layers. Beneath the mound is the original silted-in pond that was excavated into the natural soils. The canal leading in from the north extended upstream for a quarter mile (Figure 4.4).

Morefield Reservoir began as an excavated pond in the canyon where the valley floor was 500 feet wide and the tributary drainage basin area was 4.1 square miles. Based on excavations, the pond was found to have been approximately 4 feet deep in about A.D. 750, with a 50-foot diameter. A seasonal high-water table would have provided it with a variable water pool, even without any flow in the canyon bottom. However, being in the canyon bottom and in the thalweg (valley way), all of the runoff from any storm would flow into the pond along with its sediment load. It would not take long for the pond to become silted. Cleaning out the pond with digging sticks and baskets was a labor-intensive but necessary operation. Not all of the accumulated sediment would be removed, and the sediment that was removed accumulated at the pond edges. Before long, instead of

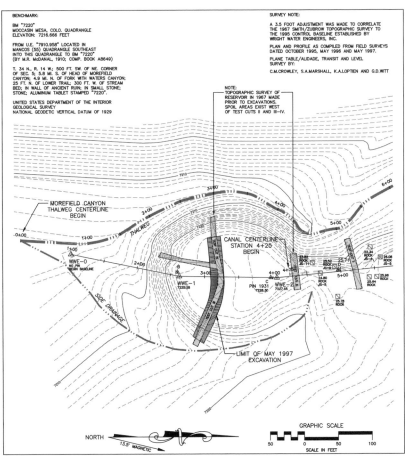

Figure 4.3: Surveys performed by our team allowed us to develop detailed topographic maps of Morefield Reservoir. (Wright Paleohydrological Institute)

merely running into the pond, occasional runoff would instead bypass the raised pond on the west.

The logical and correct reaction was to artificially divert the runoff into the pond that was now higher than the adjacent channel, just as modern water users would do. At first the canal was short; as the reservoir silt accumulated and the reservoir rose, the canal leading into it was raised and extended upstream. The canal banks were lined with shaped stones to help guard against erosion (Figure 4.5). Like other early civilizations, the Ancestral Puebloans effectively utilized hammerstones for stone shaping (Figure 4.6). There is only questionable evidence left of the final diversion point north of the mound, at the beginning point of the canal (Figure 4.7).

Figure 4.4: Ruth Wright walks on the berm route of the inlet canal that supplied water to Morefield Reservoir. Prior to the 2000 Bircher Forest Fire, the canal was hidden by sagebrush. (Ernie Pemberton)

Figure 4.5: Abundant canal stones defined the route of the inlet canal that fed Morefield Reservoir. The stones protected the canal from erosion by fast-flowing water. (Ruth Wright)

Figure 4.6: Artifacts such as this hammerstone helped identify building and operational methods used by the Ancestral Puebloans for the Morefield Reservoir public works project. (Ruth Wright)

Figure 4.7: Team members inspect a likely location of a Morefield Canyon channel diversion dam (near the trees) used to send water into the inlet canal to supply Morefield Reservoir. (Ruth Wright)

Jack Smith performed scientific excavation of the canal in 1967. His descriptions of the excavations (Figures 4.8 and 4.9) show a continuous vertical pattern of numerous canal cross-sections. Each canal section was above the last to keep pace with the increasing elevation of the reservoir, which rose with each major sediment inflow, subsequent dredging, and occasional berm building. The canal evidence was so clear that we could measure the width and depth of each cross-section and see the gravel in the bottom. The canal sequences cover an overall time period of more than three hundred years. Engineering analyses indicated that the reservoir rose 0.7 inch per year on the average; the canal had to keep up with the reservoir rise.

Archaeological Evaluation

When Smith excavated the reservoir mound in 1967, equipment limitations precluded his trenching deeper than 8 feet, although three test pits extended an additional 2 to 5 feet. Our 1997 excavations (Figure 4.10), however, achieved a depth of 16 feet by utilizing the largest hydraulic backhoe available in Montezuma County. What we found inside the mound was like stepping back in time to the A.D. 750–1100 period of the Pueblo I and II people. For instance, we could discern that on one particular day the wind had been blowing from the southwest, as indicated by ripple marks still visible on a buried sand layer (Figure 4.11). Also, on the reservoir's west bank was clear geotechnical evidence of a slope failure caused when the Ancestral

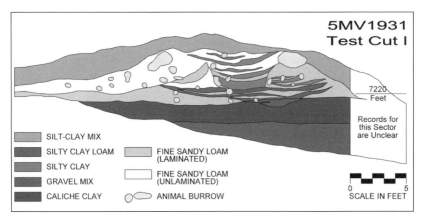

Figure 4.8: The many centuries of canal operation are illustrated in this cross-section of the berm that was developed from long periods of ditch cleaning. The dish-shaped sections represent sediment deposited in the bottom of various canals over time. (Wright Paleohydrological Institute)

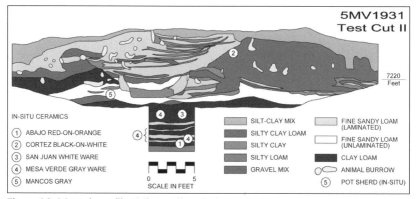

Figure 4.9: A trench profile at the north end of Morefield Reservoir shows a series of canal sections, evidenced by dish-shaped deposits of sediment that silted in the bottom of the inlet canal. It provides further documentation of the numerous canal cross-sections shown in Figure 4.8. Numbers represent locations where potsherds were found. Here the vertical height of the various elevations of the canals is nearly 12 feet. (Wright Paleohydrological Institute)

Puebloans carved the inner bank of the berm too steeply while dredging sediments, perhaps in about A.D. 900 (Figure 4.12). To a geologist or civil engineer, the evidence showed a classic earth slide complete with a rotational, downward, and easterly movement. There was even a slump block we at first thought might be the remains of a fire pit.

Potsherds throughout the excavation indicated that the reservoir dated from the Pueblo I and II periods, the Pueblo I potsherds being in the deepest strata (Figure 4.13). State archaeologist Susan Collins helped us with the scientific pottery identification. Implements such as a flat sandstone tool told us of the means of sediment excavation. A deer antler found at a depth of 13 feet had likely been used as an excavation tool. Carbon-14 testing at a University of Colorado laboratory showed that the deer antler was from about A.D. 860. A few shards on the surface and near the top of the mound were identified as Pueblo III, indicating that the reservoir had last been used in about A.D. 1100. All of this helped to explain the flat surface of the top of the mound, which had come to resemble a dance or ceremonial platform. The final inflow of water and sediment settled out uniformly over the entire pool area, resulting in a flat surface covering some 14,000 square feet.

Study of the sediment layering and its characteristics provided much evidence on environmental conditions, ways of life, and some of the problems faced by the Ancestral Puebloan public works engineers during the building and operation of the Morefield Reservoir structures. We took three con-

Figure 4.10: the team members worked in the trench from morning to night to document the south trench face evidence. A 5-foot grid system was used. Markers were used to identify the locations of sediment layering, pottery sherds, carbon-14 samples, and sediment samples that were used for gradation and pollen analysis. (Ruth Wright)

Figure 4.11: This compacted sand layer from the Morefield Reservoir deposits shows ripples caused by the wind blowing from the southwest on a particular day in the ninth century. (Ruth Wright)

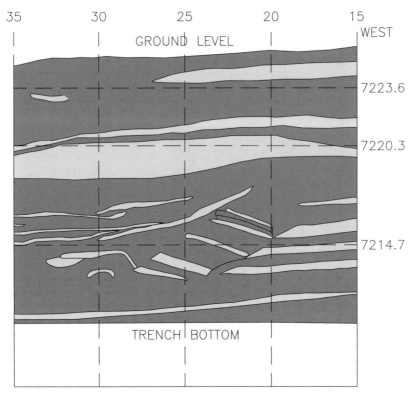

Figure 4.12: This remarkable reservoir sediment layering shows a prehistoric berm failure with a classical slip plane. The Ancestral Puebloans trimmed the Morefield Reservoir berm too steeply, causing it to collapse with a downward slide. They went on with their work of storing water, as evidenced by the sand layer sloping upward from left to right. (Wright Paleohydrological Institute)

tinuous soil profiles down the south trench wall (Figure 4.14), with one complete profile being analyzed by the Natural Resources and Conservation Service field office in Cortez for listing in its national database.

The soil profile data provided solid evidence that the reservoir was watertight because of the dense clays that were deposited there, the type of clay that modern engineers might use for solid-waste site designs to preclude leaching. We also learned that over the life of the reservoir, some fourteen forest fires had resulted in ash deposits, as shown by continuous thin layers of carbon about one-thirty-second to one-sixteenth of an inch thick. The sediments also provided evidence of twenty-one periods of high flow in the canyon bottom, as shown by thick, sandy sediment deposits, though many of the thickest sand deposits were also highly stratified, indi-

0 1 2 3

SCALE IN INCHES

Figure 4.13: Pieces of pottery were found in the excavation of the wall of Morefield Reservoir. They provided absolute proof that people were actively involved with the reservoir operation and that the activity was during the Pueblo II period. These particular potsherds were collected during the 1967 excavation. (Jack Smith)

cating successive independent inflows of high water. The shape of the layering told us of reservoir cleaning operations, where the dredged sediment had been cast to build berms or had merely been dumped outside the berm. We also noted that sometimes one part of the reservoir had been used for storage while the other was not.

Because the trench depth was limited to 16 feet due to the density of the soil, we were able to excavate to the bottom of the mound but not to the original pond bottom. By using a hand auger in the trench bottom, we logged the sediment deposits to an additional 5 feet of depth until the auger encountered the original natural soil. We could identify the original soil because team member Doug Ramsey, a soil scientist, spent five years analyzing the natural soils of Mesa Verde. By exposing the natural undisturbed soil surface in the west and east ends of the trench and defining the pond bottom, we could sketch the likely original shape of the excavated pond that lay under the 16-foot-high mound, for a total reservoir height of 21 feet.

Figure 4.14: Natural Resources and Conservation Service soil scientist Douglas Ramsey collected three complete soil profiles from the Morefield Reservoir excavation. The samples were used for gradation analysis and for pollen testing. The evidence showed extensive upstream maize agriculture. (Ruth Wright)

Berm Building

Eric Bikis, a former oil company geologist, made a detailed analysis of the berm-building periods by using common oil field sedimentology techniques. His study of the trench profile found seven distinct reservoir periods, from the original excavated pond in A.D. 750 to the final reservoir period in A.D. 1100 (Figure 4.15). The approximate dates were assessed based on pottery evidence, carbon-14 analysis, and average sedimentation rates. The berms were clearly discernible to even an untrained eye. Our team members were ecstatic at being able to read the archaeological evidence like an open book.

The topographic mapping of the mound and its canal, coupled with the surface topography of the undisturbed adjacent land surface, allowed for total volume computations. We learned that the mound and pond contained 15,000 cubic yards of water-borne sediment, while the canal berm represented another 1,000 cubic yards for a total of 16,000 cubic yards of water-deposited sediment. This represented an average of 45 cubic yards per year. The reservoir had grown in height at the net rate of 0.7 inch per

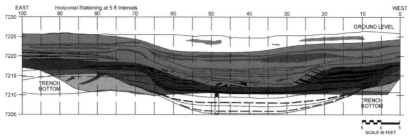

Figure 4.15: The trench wall provided details of sediment layering of Morefield Reservoir with many reservoir berm phases over its 350-year period of operation. (Wright Paleohydrological Institute)

year. When the reservoir's cleaning operations were taken into account, however, the total estimated rise in elevation was 1.6 inches per year. Ernest Pemberton computed the sediment rate as comparable to modern estimates of erosion in similar watersheds. Pemberton, now retired, was a U.S. Bureau of Reclamation reservoir sedimentation expert.

Water Yield

Our geomorphological field studies in Morefield Canyon from 1995 to 1997 showed that there had been essentially no runoff in the canyon thalweg for the past several decades (Figure 4.16). The question arose of how the mound could have been a reservoir when there had seldom been any flow to be stored. We answered that question by finding maize pollen in the reservoir sediments, proving that agricultural fields had existed upstream during prehistoric times. It is well known to hydrologists that tilled agricultural fields have more runoff than natural soils covered with grass and bushes. We also know that an occasional forest fire would greatly increase runoff, and the effects might last ten to twenty years. At the time of our field research, Morefield Canyon had not had a forest fire for at least one hundred years.

Our observations of Morefield Canyon continued from 1997 to 2000 with no evidence of much flow in the canyon thalweg. Then came the disastrous Bircher Forest Fire in July 2000 (Figure 4.17). From the time when the fire was finally controlled in August 2000 until October 2002, our observations showed frequent runoff events at the reservoir mound. It was clear that the Ancestral Puebloans had had a supply of surface water for their Morefield Reservoir because they had also had forest fires from time to time as well as the upstream agricultural land. We estimated that there would have been water for storage about five times per year.

Figure 4.16: The bottom of Morefield Canyon showed no signs of recent stream flow. Before the 2000 forest fire thick vegetation grew in the thalweg (valley way) of the canyon. After the fire this area was converted to a sand-bed ephemeral stream bottom. (Ken Wright)

Figure 4.17: The dense green forest on the Morefield Canyon walls was destroyed by the 2000 Bircher Forest Fire. Once the thick sagebrush growth on the sides and tops of Morefield Reservoir was burned off, a bare mound was visible, with a flat top that looked to some like a huge dance platform. (Ken Wright)

Geologic Framework

The research team was fortunate to have Ernest Pemberton and John Rold participate in all four of the reservoir studies. Formerly Colorado state geologist and director of the Colorado Geological Survey, Rold had investigated Morefield Canyon before the 2000 Bircher Fire, along with Pemberton and Bikis. An excerpt of his 1997 report, included as the Appendix, explains the geology of the reservoir site.

In 1998 and 1999 Pemberton, Rold, and our research team continued the inspection of Morefield Canyon's valley bottom. We noted the absence of erosion in the canyon bottom and continued lack of runoff evidence. In August and October 2000 we conducted two field inspections following the Bircher Forest Fire. There was a significant change in the watershed owing to the fire, and the erosion in the channel of Morefield Canyon was now active. What we found tended to verify Rold's 1997 description of the geomorphology. The valley bottom had recent washes of sand extending out from small gullies, and the thalweg now contained fresh sand and ash deposits that provided evidence of several flows of 15 to 30 cubic feet per second, similar to what we believed had occurred during Pueblo I and II times. The ash deposits were similar to the fourteen layers we had found earlier in the Morefield Reservoir sediment deposits, and the sand was similar in appearance to the sandy layers of the reservoir deposits. From 2001 to 2003 we made similar inspections of Morefield Canyon, uncovering similar recent sandy deposits in the valley bottom but no ash deposits. Periodic flows were still occurring in Morefield Canyon because of the changed drainage basin hydrology due to the 2000 Bircher Forest Fire. In 2004 and 2005 we noticed that ash flow had ceased, the grass was growing in the canyon bottom, and sandy sediment was no longer being regularly deposited along the thalweg.

Conclusions About Morefield Reservoir

Morefield Reservoir began as a hand-dug pond in the canyon bottom to capture seasonal groundwater. A subsequent supply of surface water was carried to the reservoir by a stone-lined canal. There was a regular series of canals, one above the other.

Sediment from the upstream drainage basin was carried to Morefield Reservoir, sometimes at a high rate. The total volume of sediment carried into the reservoir was about 430,000 cubic feet (0.0067 acre-feet per square mile per year). Morefield Reservoir was likely abandoned when dredging became too inefficient or when the Morefield people began to think about moving to cliff dwellings.

The dredged sediment used for the Morefield dam embankments was a mixture of clay, silt, and fine sand, which created a nearly impervious berm. We found that sand deposits had been cast over the top of the berm.

Based on potsherd analyses, Morefield Reservoir was used for approximately 350 years, during the A.D. 750–1100 period of the Pueblo I and II people. Over the 350-year life of the reservoir, there were about twenty-one instances of measurable sand to sandy clay deposition that represented canyon flooding and fourteen instances of thin, continuous layers of charcoal representing forest fires.

Prehistoric agricultural fields in the Morefield basin and occasional forest fires likely allowed enough runoff for the reservoir to store up to 120,000 gallons of water at a time.

5

Far View Reservoir

THE PREHISTORIC rock-walled depression on Chapin Mesa, known by millions of park visitors as Far View Reservoir, is a domestic water supply reservoir dating from A.D. 950 to 1180. This reservoir provides additional evidence of the considerable technical and planning capabilities of the early Americans of Mesa Verde. For several decades the archaeological ruin was cloaked in controversy regarding its original function—so much so, in fact, that the Park Service maintained a dual interpretive sign (Figure 5.1). One half portrayed it as an early Indian dance pavilion while the other showed it as a reservoir, with women ladling water into jars. Earlier some scientists had thought that Far View Reservoir might have been a great kiva. *National Geographic* magazine's double-page portrayal in February 1964 erroneously pictured it as part of a great irrigation system with long canals extending the length of Chapin Mesa; we found that there had been no irrigation canals. In 1969 University of Colorado field excavations by David Breternitz and Al Lancaster identified Far View Reservoir as a water storage site (Figure 5.2). Many scientists, however, remained unconvinced because there were no data to prove that the site, with its long, narrow ridge, had had even a semblance of a water supply.

In 1998 and 1999 Wright Paleohydrological Institute undertook a comprehensive paleohydrological study that not only proved the reservoir theory but also showed that the early Americans who lived some one thousand years ago in this harsh environment had been good public works engineers. The National Park Service replaced its two contradictory interpretive signs with one that renamed the site. Mummy Lake—in actuality never a lake—became Far View Reservoir (Figure 5.3).

Site Description
Far View Reservoir is centrally located on Chapin Mesa approximately 4 miles north of park headquarters and slightly more than 1 mile south of the Far View complex that houses the visitor center. The reservoir site lies 50 feet east of the main paved road at an elevation of about 7,739 feet (Figure 5.4). Far View Reservoir is one of three dozen archaeological sites open to the public. Because it is close to Far View Village, Coyote Village,

61

Figure 5.1: The earlier National Park Service interpretive sign at Far View Reservoir described two theories for the prehistoric purpose of the structure, with a final statement that "perhaps future research will answer the question." The public works engineering study did answer the question, and in 1999 the Park Service changed the sign to reflect the new findings. (Ruth Wright)

Figure 5.2: Mesa Verde legend Al Lancaster is shown surveying what he thought was an irrigation ditch leading down from Far View Reservoir. It later was judged to be a Chaco road or an early tourist access road; there was no prehistoric irrigation in Mesa Verde National Park. (National Park Service File)

Figure 5.3: The revised interpretive sign changed Mummy Lake to Far View Reservoir. It shows the site to be an Ancestral Puebloan public works project with agriculture that existed on Chapin Mesa during prehistoric periods. (Ruth Wright)

and Megalithic House—whose prehistoric inhabitants likely helped to build and maintain the reservoir—Far View Reservoir is a popular site (Figure 5.5). The plaque commemorating the designation of the four reservoir sites by the American Society of Civil Engineers as a National Historic Civil Engineering Landmark is located at Far View Reservoir (Figure 5.6).

The Far View Reservoir drainage catchment, conveyance, and storage system is about 1 mile long from north to south, including a water-gathering area at the northern end. The entire system is perched along the ridgeline of Chapin Mesa, dropping 310 feet in elevation from 8,020 feet at the north end to 7,739 feet at the Reservoir. The ridge falls off to both the east and west, and the natural soils have modest infiltration rates.

The reservoir is 90 feet in diameter, enclosed with a double rock-walled berm (Figure 5.7). The tops of the reservoir walls are 7.9 feet above the pond bottom, but water storage never exceeded a depth of 4.6 feet, representing a maximum of about 80,000 gallons of stored water. A long, sloping ramp on the west side of the enclosure likely provided access for the filling of water jars and later, perhaps, for ceremonial purposes. On the south side a formal stairway descended from the reservoir's rock-lined berm to near

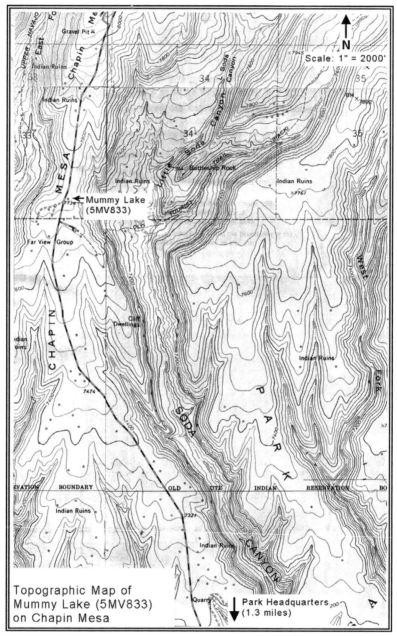

Figure 5.4: The location of Mummy Lake, now known as Far View Reservoir, is near the main tourist access road to Chapin Mesa. Millions of people have visited and enjoyed the site; it has helped to develop a better understanding of prehistoric Americans and the flourishing of the Ancestral Puebloans during the Pueblo II period of a thousand years ago. (Wright Paleohydrological Institute)

Figure 5.5: This view of Far View Reservoir shows the walled berm that provided for dredging storage. The curved stone walls to the right likely represent a ceremonial pathway down to the water pool. (John Rold)

Figure 5.6: In 2004 the American Society of Civil Engineers designated the four reservoirs at Mesa Verde National Park a National Historic Civil Engineering Landmark. The commemorative plaque is at the Far View Reservoir site. (Ruth Wright)

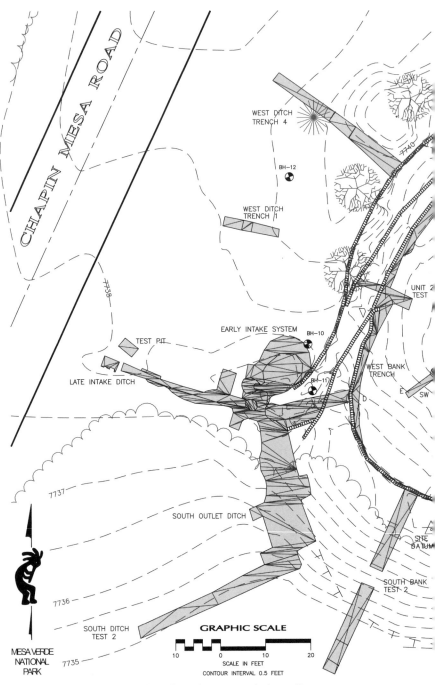

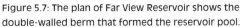

Figure 5.7: The plan of Far View Reservoir shows the
double-walled berm that formed the reservoir pool.

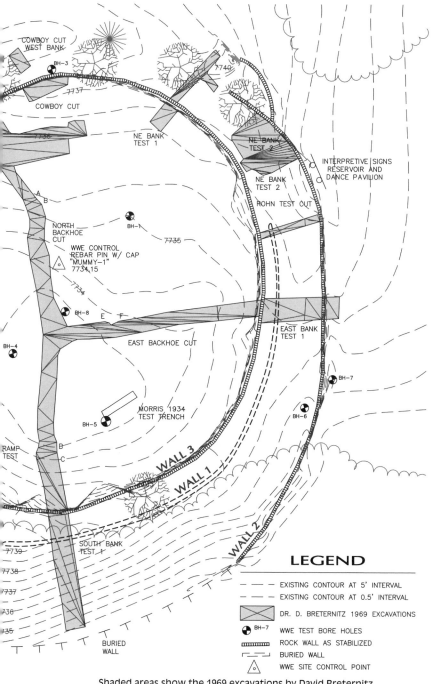

COWBOY CUT
WEST BANK
BH-3

COWBOY CUT

7737

7740

NE BANK
TEST 1

NE BANK
TEST 2

NE BANK
TEST 2

INTERPRETIVE SIGNS
RESERVOIR AND
DANCE PAVILION

ROHN TEST CUT

A B

NORTH
BACKHOE
CUT

BH-1

7735

WWE CONTROL
REBAR PIN W/ CAP
"MUMMY-1"
7734.15

7734

BH-8

E F

EAST BACKHOE CUT

EAST BANK
TEST 1

BH-4

BH-7

MORRIS 1934
TEST TRENCH

BH-5

BH-6

RAMP
TEST

B

C

WALL 3

WALL 1

WALL 2

7739

SOUTH BANK
TEST 1

7738

7737

736

735

BURIED
WALL

LEGEND

— — — EXISTING CONTOUR AT 5' INTERVAL

– – – EXISTING CONTOUR AT 0.5' INTERVAL

DR. D. BRETERNITZ 1969 EXCAVATIONS

BH-7 WWE TEST BORE HOLES

ROCK WALL AS STABILIZED

BURIED WALL

WWE SITE CONTROL POINT

Shaded areas show the 1969 excavations by David Breternitz
and Al Lancaster. (Wright Paleohydrological Institute)

the water surface, where numerous stepping-stones into the reservoir were documented in 1969 (Figure 5.8). The stairway is one of only several such structures in the national park, and its design and construction are much more elaborate than the level needed merely for utilitarian access to the water, so a special social or religious function may have been associated with the stairway (Figure 5.9). The site still has religious significance to the Hopi people, the descendants of the Ancestral Puebloans (Figure 5.10).

Investigation Procedure

The main question, and the cause of the controversy over the site's original function, was whether any water could even have flowed into Far View Reservoir. For this reason there were two special components to the paleo-hydrological research. The first was whether a water supply could be proven beyond doubt. The second was to bring experienced and credible archaeologists into the research team so that if the field evidence was con-

Figure 5.8: The Far View Reservoir stairway appears in the background in 1969, prior to restoration work by the National Park Service. In the foreground the excavation work of David Breternitz and Al Lancaster shows the stepping-stones and route down to the water's edge. (David Breternitz)

Figure 5.9: The restored stairway into Far View Reservoir shows that it was much more than a utilitarian route to the water's edge. Rather, the stairway probably had a special religious or social function. It is one of only a few such stairways in Mesa Verde National Park. (Ruth Wright)

Figure 5.10: In 2004 Michael Kabotie, a shaman representing the Ancestral Puebloans' descendants, led a Hopi prayer ceremony at Far View Reservoir. (Ruth Wright)

vincing, they could help set the record straight. We were fortunate to enlist David Breternitz, now professor emeritus at the University of Colorado; Jack Smith, the former chief archaeologist at Mesa Verde; and Calvin Cummings, former chief archaeologist, National Park Service.

During the field studies, we conducted two important water runoff analyses. The goal of the first was to identify ancient agricultural areas upslope from the reservoir, as such areas would have had an artificially high runoff. Our 1999 reservoir dredging material soil samples contained maize pollen, which proved the farming theory. For the second analysis, we observed areas around the reservoir during short rainstorms. Soil areas hard-packed from the foot traffic of site visitors were noted to be nearly impervious, whereas nearby unpacked natural soils with vegetation were judged to have very low runoff. Observations made during a modest rainfall in 1999 revealed that water flowed into Far View Reservoir from the adjacent foot traffic paths and that about 0.5 cubic yard of sediment was deposited overnight. To further support the field hydrological analyses, two early photographs obtained from Park Service archives showed cowboys watering their horses at Far View Reservoir (Figure 5.11). Water came from the old cowboy trail along the ridge of Chapin Mesa and entered the structure through the Cowboy Cut via the north berm. These findings laid the basic groundwork for further specialized and focused hydrological studies.

The hydrological and scientific procedures used at Morefield Reservoir were also employed at Far View Reservoir; however, here the palynology analysis proved of special importance because it answered other lingering questions about the prehistoric operation and maintenance of Far View Reservoir. Although the 1969 pollen samples had been taken only from the reservoir, Ruth Wright surmised that the place to collect pollen samples was the dredging dump site, between the walls. The dumping area proved to be a pollen bonanza. In addition to finding maize pollen between the stone walls, we also found shards and evidence of water-loving plants. David Breternitz, who handled the 1969 excavation of Far View Reservoir, was especially helpful to the paleohydrology research because of his personal knowledge of what lay underground at the site.

Site Characteristics

Based on the 1998–1999 Wright Paleohydrological Institute fieldwork and earlier studies, we concluded that Far View Reservoir had been constructed in three phases. The dredge sediment deposit area, between the

Figure 5.11: Far View Reservoir was used by cowboys in the early 1900s for watering their horses. The water in the reservoir at that time was obtained in the same manner used by the Ancestral Puebloans nine hundred years earlier, by collecting water from packed ground surfaces via a ditch leading into the depression through the stone wall that is now known as the Cowboy Cut. (National Park Service File)

stone walls to the east and south, provided evidence of alluvial materials (Figure 5.12) that had been dredged from the reservoir pool. During pre-historic times, sandy and clayey material was removed from the reservoir from time to time. Some of the sand was alluvium deposited in the reservoir, and a portion may have been decomposed sandstone from the underlying bedrock.

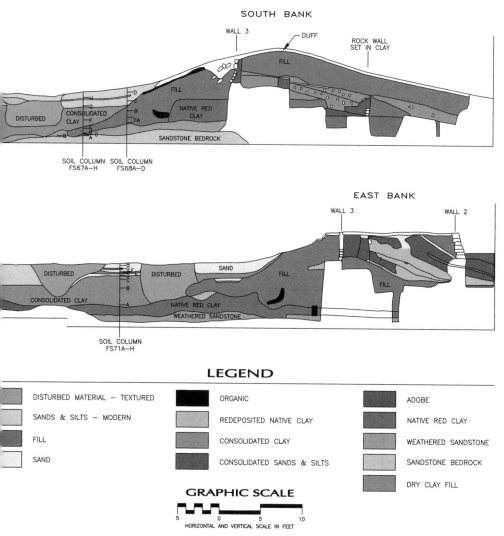

Figure 5.12: Cross-sections of Far View Reservoir by David Breternitz in 1969 show what he found in the excavations. The mound to the right in both sections represents the dredged material fill and the redeposited red clay from the original excavation. (Wright Paleohydrological Institute)

The berms and fill at Far View Reservoir represent approximately 1,100 cubic yards, roughly 200 percent of the excavated natural soils. Without taking into account wind-deposited sediments, the sediment volume at Far View Reservoir indicates an average inflow of sediment of about 2.4 cubic yards per year over 230 years from A.D. 950 to 1180. Wind and water erosion of the banks, if considered, would tend to raise the estimate of this sedimentation rate. Owing to the sandstone bedrock and native clay loam of the soil, the reservoir would have been relatively watertight.

Based on a 1973 pollen testing report, we concluded that existing Far View Reservoir sediment deposits include both reservoir occupational (before A.D. 1180) and postoperational (after A.D. 1180) sediments. For instance, *Zea* (maize) pollen recovered in two soil samples indicated operational sediments at the site, low in the vertical soil profile near the bedrock. Based on the resource evaluation and surveys of the water-gathering area of an estimated 25 acres, including pollen testing, we concluded that the water-gathering area was capable of producing occasional surface runoff from packed-down and farmed areas (maize).

A footpath from the Far View Reservoir area, following the approximate ridgeline upslope to the water-gathering area (cornfield), would have been capable of transporting surface runoff to Far View Reservoir with only minor losses. The footpath would have served as a canal. Based on a study of average precipitation patterns during the winter (December to March), we concluded that snowpack would usually accumulate in Far View Reservoir, creating snowmelt water in mid-April amounting in depth to anywhere from a few inches to as much as 1.5 feet. From analyses of the soil character, geology, and monthly precipitation amounts, we concluded that there was no permanent water table on Chapin Mesa; a perched water table on top of the clay layer or at the soil/sandstone contact level would occur very infrequently. A perched water table could cause groundwater flow into Far View Reservoir along the surface of the red clay layer or on top of the sandstone bedrock.

During 1999 the three piezometers that we installed in Far View Reservoir remained dry; however, the 1998–1999 winter was dry, and the April 1999 rains on Chapin Mesa totaled only 2.13 inches. Thus, a perched water table source to Far View Reservoir has been discounted; even by 2005, the piezometers remained dry.

Final Assessment of Far View Reservoir

Finally, after weighing all the available data, we concluded that Far View Reservoir had been initiated in about A.D. 950 as a simple excavation without walls for the purpose of occasionally storing domestic water. Groundwater was not a water source for the reservoir. The water source was from the melting of the spring snowpack and occasional surface runoff.

An old route from Far View Reservoir southward down Chapin Mesa toward the park headquarters or Cliff Palace was not a former irrigation ditch. The route was likely an early Park Service roadway. There was never an ancient irrigation ditch known as Far View Ditch.

The three stone walls of Far View Reservoir were built to retain dredged sediment. One wall is buried under the surrounding embankment.

The 25-acre area (water-gathering basin) lying 1 mile north of Far View Reservoir was an agricultural field during the Pueblo II period. As a result, rainfall-runoff characteristics caused surface runoff several times each year. Runoff water could have been carried from the field to Far View Reservoir via a foot-packed trail, and later a canal.

The potential ditches examined in the northerly water-gathering basin were likely modern natural flow paths created by runoff flowing downslope at right angles to the contour lines, rather than human-made ditches.

The high-status stone stairway leading into Far View Reservoir is one of only a few known to exist in the park. Another is at the nearby Pipe Shrine House. The stairway at Far View Reservoir is not an essential part of an ancient water storage facility; however, it provided good access from the embankment to the potential water body.

The purpose and function of Far View Reservoir from A.D. 950 to 1180 was for periodic domestic water storage. Much of the time it would have had no water and, therefore, it provided an infrequent and unreliable source of water for the early inhabitants.

We were not able to adequately explain the enigmatic circular structure, excavated by Al Lancaster, southwest of the reservoir that had been thought to be the early intake where sediment would settle (Figure 5.13).

Figure 5.13: The final enigma for the public works paleohydrologists is the function of this early structure at Far View Reservoir. The 1969 excavators considered it to be the "early intake" that would cause sediment to settle prior to storage. Additional studies are needed to define its function and to resolve this question. (David Breternitz)

6

Sagebrush Reservoir

THE MESA-TOP RESERVOIR site now called Sagebrush Reservoir is 1 mile west of Chapin Mesa and Far View Reservoir. The reservoir site features two intersecting trenches across its surface cut by Jack Smith and his University of Colorado archaeology team in 1972–1974, with a D-shaped berm (Figure 6.1). The northwest wall of the berm has an opening onto the adjacent mesa top. The site looks nothing like a reservoir location.

In sharp contrast to the sizable population supported by Chapin Mesa with the population centers of Far View Village, Coyote Village, and Pipe Shrine House, this mesa was lightly populated. The mesa, which even now remains unnamed, is further separated from Chapin Mesa by the 500-foot-deep, steeply sloping East Fork Navajo Canyon. Near the canyon bottom is a small spring that maintains a water trickle; it was a long trip for the water-gathering women. Certainly a reservoir on the mesa top would have been desirable.

In about A.D. 950 the Pueblo II residents selected a location for collecting and storing supplemental water on the narrow mesa top on an east-west line with Morefield and Far View Reservoirs, where the north-south ground surface gradient was slightly less than to the north (2 percent vs. 3 percent). An initial pond excavation was made into the sterile silt clay loam to a depth of about 4 feet and with a diameter of some 30 feet, for a total excavated volume of 60 cubic yards, enough to reasonably store 12,000 gallons. The site lay 70 feet south of the pueblo that is designated 5MV2236 (Figure 6.2). However, a hole in the ground does not create storage; there must be a water source.

Paleohydrological studies show that no water would have flowed into the pond without human intervention. As a result, the Ancestral Puebloans had to have constructed an interceptor ditch collection system that fed into the pond from the north. Archaeological excavations in 1972–1974 showed fine, laminated, hard-packed sands nearly a foot thick with dredged material at the edges; the sands in the ponding area were water borne, and the artifacts found in the sand layer prove human activity. Pueblo II artifacts helped date the reservoir site.

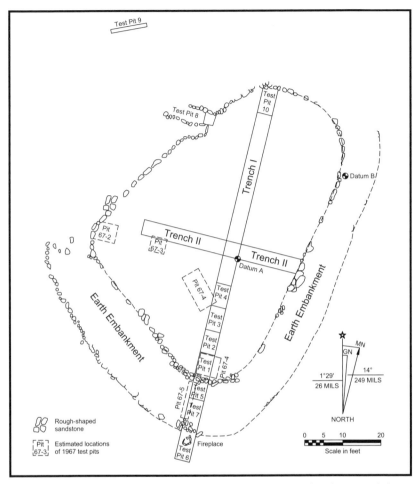

Figure 6.1: Plan of the 1972–1974 excavations at Site 5MV1936, Sagebrush Reservoir, by Dr. Jack Smith. (Wright Paleohydrological Institute)

The pond excavation was extensive given the digging sticks and baskets and other simple tools in use at that time. Over the next one hundred or so years, the reservoir would include two more phases, and the storage would increase to about 40,000 gallons. Sediment and artifacts would be deposited and, over time, the reservoir would become mostly silted. Finally, in about A.D. 1100, the reservoir function was terminated. Perhaps it was too hard to maintain. That people continued to use the site for other purposes is evident by potsherds in top-layer eolian deposits.

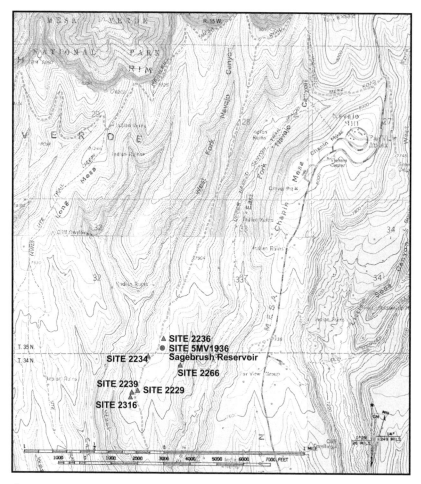

Figure 6.2: Archaeological sites in proximity to Site 5MV1936, Sagebrush Reservoir. (Wright Paleohydrological Institute)

The upper-strata material was transported not by water but by wind (Figure 6.3).

Water Yield of Surface Soil

Initially we called the reservoir Stone Axe after an axe head found at the site (Figure 6.4). *Zea mays* pollen collected from the dredged material in the berm and from three of the reservoir's sediment strata confirmed corn farming near the site. In the prehistoric period, however, *Artemisia* (sagebrush) was by far the dominant plant. Hence, the site was renamed.

Figure 6.3: Excavations by Dr. Jack Smith at Sagebrush Reservoir in 1972–1974 resulted in an important cross-section of the reservoir deposits that showed stepping-stones, tools, pottery, and even a metate. (Jack Smith)

Figure 6.1 shows the reservoir in plan view. Figure 6.5 shows contours through the reservoir. Figure 6.2 shows its relation to adjacent settlements and area-wide topography.

As with Far View Reservoir, the lack of any natural drainage basin left doubts about the function of the structure. Even though the specific deposits in the structures were proven to be water borne, and even though artifacts in the sediments proved there had been human intervention and participation, scientists would continue to question the reservoir theory if the team failed to prove a water supply.

The problem was resolved by using a simple field hydraulic model of tamped and wetted bare earth on a game trail. A small area was tamped with fingers and thumb to represent a one-half-acre site subject to the foot traffic of the Pueblo II inhabitants. Then a small canal was connected to a simulated reservoir depression. For test purposes, small amounts of water were applied elsewhere to the normal game trail surface, where the water quickly infiltrated and was lost. Next, water was applied to the simulated drainage basin, where it immediately accumulated, ran down the canal, and filled the simulated reservoir (Figure 6.6). Due to the high percentage of silt and clay in the eolian surface deposit, puddling of the soil brought the

Figure 6.4: Ken Wright holds a stone axe that was found near Sagebrush Reservoir. It was lying on the open ground, where it had been dropped about a thousand years before. The indentation in the ground surface was only about one-eighth inch, indicating that little windblown soil had been deposited on the mesa since the abandonment of the community there. (Ruth Wright)

fine particles to the surface to form a nearly impervious cover that caused the immediate runoff. We had each of the archaeologist team members pour water and observe its accumulation in the simulated reservoir.

We concluded that human alteration of small surface areas of the mesa topsoil, perhaps even an area as small as half an acre, would provide adequate runoff during a 0.5-inch or less rainfall in an hour.

The Excavation Profile

The north-south and east-west profiles excavated by the University of Colorado team provided detailed evidence of the reservoir building, operation, types of various sediment layers, pieces of pottery, stepping-stones, and even a metate (Figure 6.7). The excavation (Trench I) profile provided evidence that the reservoir had three phases; see the Phase 1, 2, and 3 north reservoir banks that resulted from sediment filling of the storage pool. The profiles also show deposits of dredged material cast to the edges in Phase 1. Locations of pollen samples are shown in two profiles.

The reddish sand in Layer II is remarkable because it extends from the far south all the way to the north Phase 3 bank. Layer I is unique because

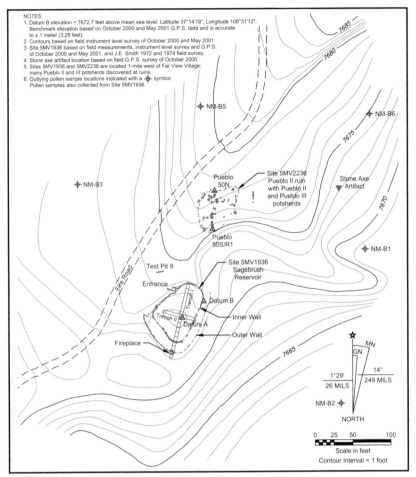

NOTES:
1. Datum B elevation = 7672.7 feet above mean sea level. Latitude 37°14'18", Longitude 108°31'12".
   Benchmark elevation based on October 2000 and May 2001 G.P.S. data and is accurate
   to ± 1 meter (3.28 feet).
2. Contours based on field instrument level survey of October 2000 and May 2001.
3. Site 5MV1936 based on field measurements, instrument level survey and G.P.S.
   of October 2000 and May 2001, and J.E. Smith 1972 and 1974 field survey.
4. Stone axe artifact location based on field G.P.S. survey of October 2000.
5. Sites 5MV1936 and 5MV2236 are located 1-mile west of Far View Village;
   many Pueblo II and III potsherds discovered at ruins.
6. Outlying pollen sample locations indicated with a ⊕ symbol.
   Pollen samples also collected from Site 5MV1936.

Figure 6.5: Vicinity contour map of Site 5MV1936, Sagebrush Reservoir.
(Wright Paleohydrological Institute)

it was deposited by wind, not water, yet it contains cultural material such as a metate, potsherds, and stones. Layer I is situated between the perimeter walls. Just outside the outer south wall is a fire pit with charcoal.

Trench II is a profile of the east-west trench, the location of which is shown on the Trench I profile. This profile shows Phase 2 and 3 reservoir banks and many details of the north trench wall showing areas disturbed by human activity, mixed sediments, potsherds, and truncated layers related to dredging.

Water entered the reservoir from the north (right) end of the reservoir. During Phase 3 the walls were constructed at the south end to provide additional storage volume because Layer II and/or Layer III had already

Figure 6.6: This simple yet effective hydraulic model proved the hypothesis that packing of a wetted and bare ground surface by the feet of the prehistoric people would change the rainfall-runoff character of the soil surface enough to create substantial runoff. The area on the left represents .5 acre of modified ground surface, while the depression on the right represents Sagebrush Reservoir. (Ruth Wright)

filled most of the available space. During the reservoir's postoperational period, when Layer I was deposited, people were using the structure for some other purpose (a social or religious use) because cultural material was deposited along with the wind-blown soil.

Paleohydrology Findings at Sagebrush Reservoir

The reservoir research found that sediments were water deposited except for Layer I, which is an eolian deposit. The sediment layers range from clay to those having a high percentage of sand; one layer was 70 percent sand. Sediment layers having large percentages of sand represent more intensive rainy periods, when soil erosion would occur. Some thicker sand layers were stratified, indicating many intense rainfall events, with each event laying down a thin layer of sediment. The clayey layers represent routine low-rainfall periods, when silt and clay would be carried into the reservoir for slow deposition.

The Sagebrush Reservoir was constructed in three phases, as evidenced by three distinct bank characteristics as shown in Figure 6.7. The capacity

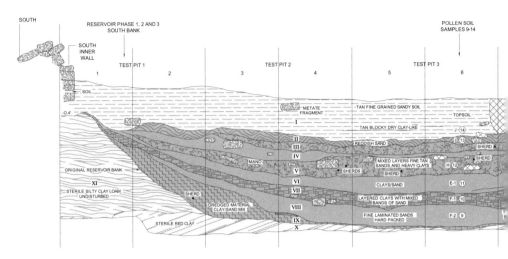

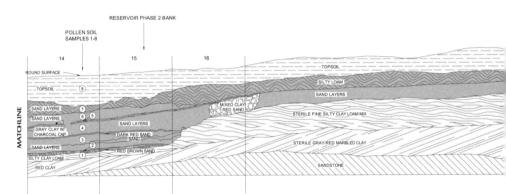

Figure 6.7: Scaled drawing of the north-south and east-west profiles of Sagebrush Reservoir, excavated by Dr. Jack Smith of the University of Colorado. (Wright Paleohydrological Institute)

LEGEND

DESCRIPTIONS BY NRCS

I	BLOCKY SILTY CLAY LOAM		MIXED SEDIMENTS
II	SILTY LOAM WITH SOME CLAY SAND NOTED IN FIELD		SILTY CLAY LOAM EXCAVATED MATERIAL FROM RESERVOIR WITH CHARCOAL TRACES
III,V	SILTY CLAY LOAM		
IV,VI,VIII	FINE SAND AND SILT		SANDSTONE
VII	FINE SILT - CLAY LOAM MIX		ROCK/STONE
IX	DREDGED DEPOSIT SILT - CLAY MIX	•	SHERD LOCATION
X	STERILE RED CLAY		
XI	STERILE SILTY CLAY LOAM		

LAYER	ARTIFACTS	CHARACTER
I	YES	POST RESERVOIR USE PER
II	YES	LONGEST CONTINUAL LAYE
III	YES	NUMEROUS LAYERING
IV	NONE	-
V	YES	-
VI	NONE	MIXED FINE SANDS AND HE
VII	YES	LAYERED CLAYS WITH MIXE
VIII	YES	FINELY LAMINATED SANDS
IX	YES	DREDGED DEPOSIT
X	NONE	ORIGINAL RED CLAY LAYER
XI	NONE	ORIGINAL SOIL, UNDISTURE
-	-	BEDROCK

1. RESERVOIR FUNCTION PERIOD, AD 950-1100.
2. PUEBLO II TO EARLY PUEBLO III.
3. 969 POTSHERDS COLLECTED.
4. SEDIMENTS WATER DEPOSITED EXCEPT FOR LAYER I.
5. NO NATURAL WATER SUPPLY, INTERCEPTOR DITCHES REQUIRED.

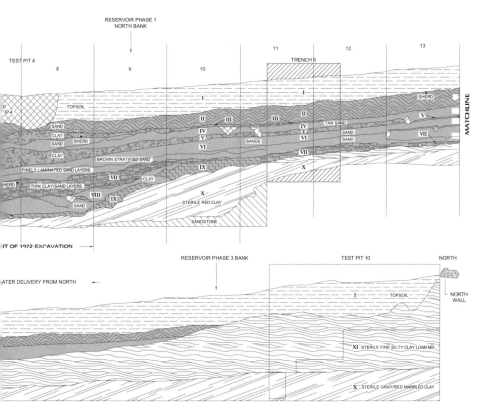

RESERVOIR PHASE 1
NORTH BANK

TEST PIT 4

8   9   10   11   TRENCH II   12   13

MATCHLINE

TOPSOIL

SAND
CLAY
SAND   SHERD
CLAY
BROWN STRATIFIED SAND
FINELY LAMINATED SAND LAYERS
THIN CLAY/SAND LAYERS
SHERD   SAND

I
II   III   III   TAN SAND   V   SHERD
IV   IV   IV
V   VI   VI   SAND   VII
VI   VII   SAND
SANDS
IX   X   SHERD
X
STERILE RED CLAY

VII   CLAY
VIII   IX

SANDSTONE

LIMIT OF 1972 EXCAVATION

RESERVOIR PHASE 3 BANK   TEST PIT 10   NORTH

WATER DELIVERY FROM NORTH

I   TOPSOIL   NORTH WALL

XI   STERILE FINE SILTY CLAY LOAM MIX

X   STERILE GRAY/RED MARBLED CLAY

GRAPHIC SCALE
1   0   1

POLLEN MAIZE	SOIL NOTES
-	SILTY CLAY LOAM ELOIAN DEPOSIT
-	SILTY LOAM WITH SOME CLAY
-	34% SAND - SILTY CLAY LOAM
YES	FINE SILT
-	17% SAND, SILTY CLAY LOAM
-	70% SAND, FINE SILT
YES	21% SAND
-	FINE SAND AND SILT
-	SILTY CLAY LOAM
-	CLAY, ORIGINAL DEPOSIT
-	SILTY CLAY LOAM, ORIGINAL
-	SANDSTONE

...IVE LAYERS OFTEN CONTAIN FINE LAMINATIONS.
...RVOIR BUILT IN THREE DISTINCT PHASES.
...S CONSTRUCTED IN PHASE III, OR LATER.
...E POLLEN FOUND BETWEEN DOUBLE WALLS TO
...HWEST. MAIZE POLLEN FOUND IN LAYERS
... VII.

NAVAJO MESA
SITE 5MV1936
SAGEBRUSH RESERVOIR SITE

PROFILES OF SHALLOW EXCAVATIONS
OF A PREHISTORIC RESERVOIR

1972 - National Park Service
1974 - University of Colorado
(Jack E. Smith - Archaeologist)

Prepared by Wright Water Engineers, Inc.

of the reservoir approximated 12,000, 16,000, and 90,000 gallons, respectively, for Phases I, II, and III. The total excavation for Sagebrush Reservoir was 180 cubic yards. During its operational period, there were about 233 cubic yards of sediment deposited in the reservoir, or about 1.5 cubic yards of sediment per year.

The reservoir berm, as it exists today, was built during Phase III. The southerly portion of the berm was raised above the natural earth surface, tending to balance the higher reservoir edge to the north. The south berm represents about 2.4 feet of elevation gain, allowing for a significant increase in the storage volume. This construction provides evidence of good engineering, knowledge of water containment principles, and the ability to work within the natural constraints of elevation differences. The berm contains about 130 cubic yards of fill material.

The mesa top was capable of generating water for Sagebrush Reservoir, even though it is not capable of doing so in modern times. No water would have reached the reservoir without human intervention. The interceptor ditches leading to the reservoir collected sediment from soil surface erosion and carried the sediment into the reservoir, where it was deposited in layers, a little at a time. A relatively small (0.5-acre) tract of agricultural land or a small (0.25-acre) area of tramped-down, unvegetated soil would generate sufficient and frequent enough water to suitably support a water storage structure and its function. Sufficient runoff for storage might typically occur five or six times per year. We proved the runoff potential of a human-modified soil surface via a series of hydraulic model tests. The prehistoric precipitation character during the Sagebrush Reservoir operation period was reasonably similar to the modern average (about 18 inches per year). Higher-intensity rainfalls (1 or 2 inches per hour) lasting five or ten minutes over a modified soil surface of only a quarter-acre would yield 5,000 to 10,000 gallons of runoff water.

Sagebrush Reservoir was initiated in about A.D. 950, at approximately the same time as Far View Reservoir. It originally had no walls and consisted of a small excavation about 26 feet in diameter and 4.3 feet in depth. Later it was enlarged to 46 feet in north-south length, but because of earlier sedimentation, it was then only 3 feet deep. Enlargement during Phase III took the north-south dimension within the walls to 77 feet, with a maximum depth of 5.2 feet. Although the Phase III reservoir itself was 77 feet from north to south, the overall size of the structure from north to south is about 90 feet when the outside perimeter wall is considered. The

D-shaped form of the reservoir reflects the natural topography of the site, which falls off to the east-southeast.

Table 6.1 provides data on the layering and potsherds found at the reservoir. Layer IX, the lowest and earliest evidence of water-deposited sediments, had been dredged. Where it was deep and thin, two shards of plain Grayware were recovered in 1974, but where it was thick, sixty-five shards were recovered, including twelve that were chronologically significant because they were of the Ackmen phase, representing the period of A.D. 900–1000. Therefore, Layer IX must have originated no earlier than A.D. 900 and been deposited during the Pueblo II period.

Layers IV, VI, and X contained no artifacts. However, Layers I, II, III, V, VII, VIII, and IX did contain artifacts.

Conclusions About Sagebrush Reservoir

Based on the paleohydrological investigations and the parallel archaeological interpretation by a team of well-seasoned and experienced scientists, we concluded that Sagebrush Reservoir consisted of an enclosure defined by a stone-faced earthen embankment on its southwest, south, and east sides and that it served a Pueblo II water storage function from about A.D. 950 to 1100.

The Sagebrush Reservoir structure ceased functioning as a reservoir before the late Pueblo II or early Pueblo III occupants abandoned the mesa top. The uppermost layer in the reservoir was not deposited by water, but it does contain evidence of human activity, such as a metate fragment. Most of the shards from Sagebrush Reservoir were from jars, with a few bowls. No dippers, mugs, or other shapes were recognized.

The opening in the northwest wall of Sagebrush Reservoir was an entranceway to the reservoir; it did not serve to convey water.

Maize pollen was found in layers II, V, and VII within the reservoir and from the area between the two walls at a depth of 17 to 20 inches, the only pollen sample tested from the berm fill.

Sagebrush Reservoir served as a useful water supply during its period of operation, providing stored water on the average of perhaps five or six times per year. The similarities with Far View Reservoir are numerous.

The Pueblo II people of the unnamed mesa were good at water harvesting and were able to build and maintain a public works project that required considerable effort and diligence over a long period of time.

			Maize	
Layer	Artifacts	Character	Pollen	Soil Notes
I	Yes	Postreservoir use period		Silty clay loam eolian deposit
II	Yes	Longest continual layer		Silty loam with some clay
III	Yes	Numerous layering		34% sand— silty clay loam
IV	None		Yes	Fine silt
V	Yes			17% sand, silty clay loam
VI	None	Mixed fine sands and heavy clays		70% sand, fine silt
VII	Yes	Layered clays with mixed bands of sand	Yes	21% sand
VIII	Yes	Finely laminated sands		Fine sand and silt
IX	Yes	Dredged deposit		Silty clay loam
X	None	Original red clay layer, undisturbed		Clay, original deposit
XI	None	Original soil, undisturbed		Silty clay loam, original
		Bedrock		Sandstone

Table 6.1
Potsherd Dating

7

Box Elder Reservoir

BOX ELDER RESERVOIR lay hidden under sagebrush in Prater Canyon for some ten centuries. Prater Canyon lies just 0.7 mile to the west of Morefield Canyon, with a high ridge between. The two canyons are similar in shape, size, and vegetation. During the earlier days of Mesa Verde National Park, the tourist road access to Chapin Mesa was down Morefield Canyon, up over the ridge, and down into lower Prater Canyon. Where the road reached the canyon bottom, there was a grove of box elder trees and a mound that went unnoticed because of a heavy growth of large sagebrush. No one knew until 2001 that the sagebrush hid a prehistoric reservoir of the Pueblo I period, even though the mound is only about 200 feet from the old road.

Once the tourist road was replaced with the new paved access road and a vehicular tunnel through the ridge that separated the two canyons, the old road into lower Prater Canyon was abandoned. Now lower Prater Canyon is remote and off-limits to the public. It is visited only infrequently, even by Mesa Verde National Park staff.

The Bircher Forest Fire of July 2000 burned Prater Canyon badly; it was a severe fire. Once the thick growth of sagebrush was burned off, the mound became apparent during the summer of 2001, when fire remediation crew supervisor Tom Shine noted the anomalous shape on the canyon-bottom terrace. Then, on September 6, 2001, Park Ranger Archaeologist James Kleidon turned his attention to the mound, its first examination in over one thousand years.

Kleidon was familiar with our research work in nearby Morefield Canyon and immediately recognized surface similarities between the Morefield mound and the Prater Canyon mound; he knew it had been a reservoir!

Kleidon made a reconnaissance survey of the Prater Canyon mound and recorded its surface pottery, shape, and dimensions. He accurately described the reservoir and judged it to be from the Pueblo I period. A year later, in 2002, Wright Paleohydrological Institute sought and received a permit from Mesa Verde National Park for an intensive field study of this newly discovered reservoir site. Our fieldwork extended into the spring of 2003.

Box Elder was the fourth reservoir studied by Wright Paleohydrological Institute/Wright Water Engineers, Inc., and the second located in a canyon. Therefore, we had a good plan for obtaining the most useful data and most knowledgeable interpretations. Once again we brought in such experts as the U.S. Bureau of Reclamation former chief sedimentation engineer Ernest Pemberton, former Colorado state geologist John Rold, archaeologist Dave Breternitz, archaeologist Jack Smith, and Quaternary geologist Mary Gillam. Some other team members joined us, including Natural Resources Conservation Service soil scientist Doug Ramsey and U.S. Bureau of Reclamation geotechnical engineer Richard Wiltshire, who assisted with the power augering; Kleidon, who advised us; groundwater expert Peter Monkmeyer; Colorado Supreme Court justice Gregory Hobbs; and Bobbie Hobbs.

With this extensive team, joined by all the usual scientists, engineers, and technicians from Wright Water Engineers, Inc., we were able to use our field time to good advantage. Crews surveyed the mound and canyon; Breternitz evaluated potsherds; field inspections were performed; the reservoir was power-augered (Figure 7.1) to analyze strata character, stratification, and thickness; hand-augered samples were taken for pollen analyses and sedimentation; and a myriad of other issues were delved, including geology, geomorphology, depth to groundwater, soil infiltration, pinpointing of key locations using a global positioning system (GPS), adjacent pueblos, technology transfer from Morefield, rainfall/runoff, and effects of the 2000 Bircher Forest Fire.

Specific Features of Box Elder Reservoir

Box Elder Reservoir is an anomalous topographic feature, a mound rising some 15 to 20 feet above the incised channel to the east. It is approximately 200 feet wide from east to west and 250 feet long from north to south. The mound has a nearly flat top, approximately 120 feet wide and 160 feet long. It merges to the north-northwest with the gently sloping valley terrace.

Prater Canyon, as shown in Figure 7.2, is a broad, U-shaped valley. Side ridges rise 500 to 600 feet on each side of the relatively flat bottom, which ranges from 500 to 1,100 feet in width. At the 5MV4505 archaeological site, the valley bottom is approximately 800 feet wide.

Figures 7.3 and 7.4 show that a nearly flat-bottomed channel, 40 to 60 feet wide and 6 to 8 feet deep, has eroded into the broad valley floor, forming flanking terraces on each side of the canyon thalweg channel. The

Figure 7.1: The U.S. Bureau of Reclamation power auger is shown being operated by Richard Wiltshire and David Breternitz to penetrate more than 20 feet of Box Elder sediment deposition before encountering natural, in situ soil. (Ruth Wright)

Figure 7.2: The Prater Valley canyon looking northward following the 2000 Bircher Forest Fire. (Ken Wright)

channel edges form vegetated, well-healed gentle slopes (see Figures 7.3 and 7.4). Prior to the 2000 Bircher fire, grass, mature sagebrush, and occasional Gambel's oak thickets covered the channel bottom and its well-rounded shoulders. A unique stand of box elder trees juts up from the channel near the mound.

The drainage basin of Prater Canyon upstream of Box Elder Reservoir covers nearly 4 square miles and ranges in elevation from 7,250 to 8,400 feet over a distance of 5 miles. The basin is forested with piñon and juniper, except for the canyon floor. We performed topographic field

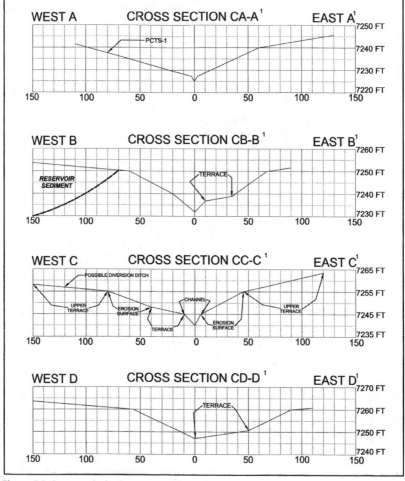

Figure 7.3: Geomorphologic cross-sections of Prater Canyon. See Figure 7.4 for locations of cross sections. (Wright Paleohyrdological Institute)

surveys with 1-foot contour lines over a wide area to better define the reservoir mound, the Prater Canyon thalweg corridor, and the likely alignment of the final water intake canal.

The Box Elder canyon floor reservoir had many physical and cultural similarities to Morefield Reservoir, including a raised mound filled with layers of water-borne deposits and an inlet canal that was extended upstream as the reservoir's elevation increased due to sediment inflow. Potsherds from the Pueblo I period (A.D. 750–900) lie on the outside surface of the U-shaped berm as a result of subtle surface erosion. It would appear that Box Elder Reservoir benefited from the success of technology transfer from people of the adjacent valley that held Morefield Reservoir.

About Box Elder Reservoir

The water storage facility in Prater Canyon did not evolve on its own; prehistoric people caused it to happen about A.D. 800, around the time that Morefield Reservoir was rising up and out of the canyon floor after about fifty years of operation.

The people of Prater Canyon needed to supplement the likely groundwater supply, which would have been derived from shallow excavations in the canyon bottom. First they went upstream about 0.7 mile from their main village area and, using digging sticks, antlers, flat stones, and baskets, excavated a pond-like hole lower and to the west of the then existing canyon thalweg to capture groundwater. Later they opened the east side of the pond to the canyon thalweg, as shown in Figure 7.5.

Water from likely field runoff and from the canyon thalweg brought with it sediment that often filled the excavation; dredging occurred, but the reservoir was not completely dredged out to the original bottom. After sediment deposition from many runoff events, the pond bottom was somewhat higher than the adjacent thalweg, which was degrading, and runoff water needed to be physically diverted into the pond. Soon a longer, formalized canal was constructed to divert the surface water flow into the rising pond. It was not many years before a new inlet canal was needed that was higher in elevation and that extended farther upstream (Figure 7.6). This process continued for perhaps well over a century, and with each canal rebuilding and upstream extension, the work needed per gallon of water increased. Soon filling the reservoir likely required more energy than the water was worth. Besides, spring and thalweg excavations elsewhere were able to provide for basic water needs for the succeeding Pueblo people.

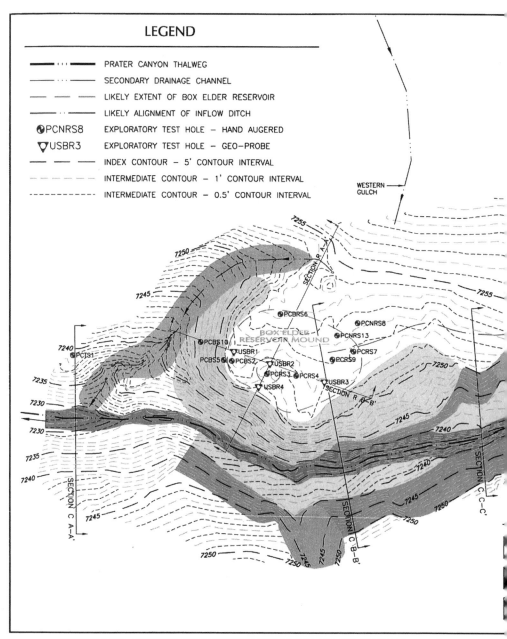

Figure 7.4: Map of Box Elder Reservoir area with shading showing the time frame of geomorphological development in Prater Canyon. (Wright Paleohyrdological Institute)

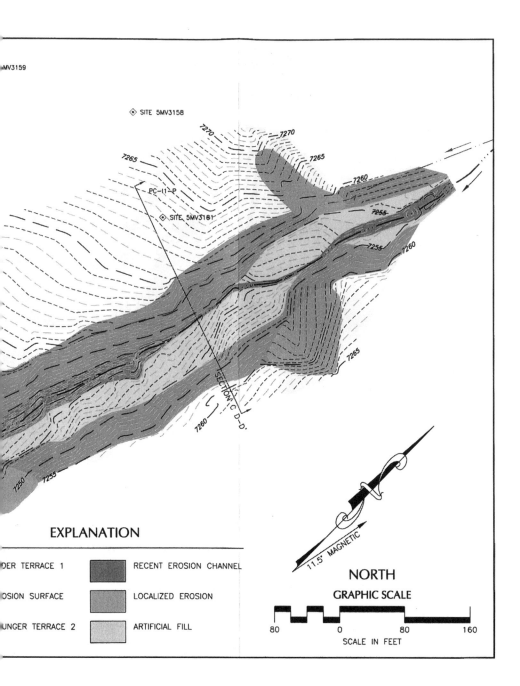

MV3159

◇ SITE 5MV3158

7270

7270

7265

7265

7260

PC-11-P

◇ SITE 5MV3161

7255

7255

7260

7265

SECTION C D-D'

7260

7250 7255

EXPLANATION

DER TERRACE 1	▓▓	RECENT EROSION CHANNEL
OSION SURFACE	▓▓	LOCALIZED EROSION
UNGER TERRACE 2	▓▓	ARTIFICIAL FILL

11.5 MAGNETIC

NORTH

GRAPHIC SCALE

80   0   80   160

SCALE IN FEET

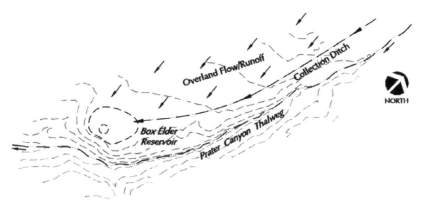

Figure 7.5: The early-phase water supply hypothesis is that overland flow from agricultural fields was collected in a ditch feeding Box Elder Reservoir to supplement groundwater in the pond bottom. (Wright Paleohyrdological Institute)

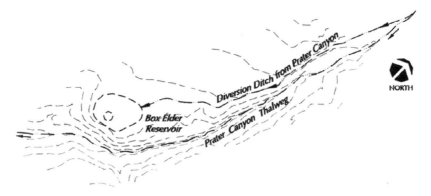

Figure 7.6: A later-phase water supply hypothesis is that a drainage ditch was developed to capture flows from Prater Canyon. (Wright Paleohyrdological Institute)

The final years of the reservoir operation likely represented sporadic diversion of the water of the canyon-wall gulch, lying to the west, into the by then raised mound on the west side of the Prater Canyon valley floor (Figure 7.7). The gulch carried much sediment into the reservoir and began filling the remaining reservoir storage space from west to east. Finally, in about A.D. 950, the Prater Canyon reservoir was abandoned in the general shape and condition it is still in today, with a reservoir surface that slopes at 3.8 percent from west to east. Subsequent runoff has caused an erosion gully on the eastern edge of the mound. The steep slope of the reservoir berm has also slowly eroded, exposing potsherds on its sloping surface.

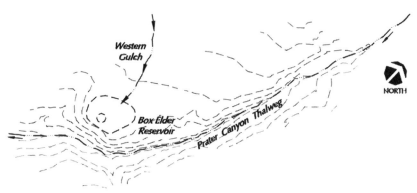

Figure 7.7: A final-phase water supply hypothesis is that Box Elder Reservoir was fed by sporadic flow from a western gulch. (Wright Paleohyrdological Institute)

Dating of Box Elder Reservoir was performed by analyzing the evidence, observing the physical characteristics of the site and valley, and tapping into the rich storehouse of ceramic information developed by Southwest archaeologists and anthropologists. The time period of the Box Elder Reservoir was determined by David Breternitz. Table 7.1 is a summary of what may have been the phases of Box Elder Reservoir, based on all of our evidence.

Prater Canyon Canal Alignment

We performed canal alignment field inspections to attempt to locate and define evidence of the intake canal at the time of abandonment. By following a hypothetical but typical 1 percent ditch slope northward from the reservoir to intercept the canyon floor channel area, team members were able to find only limited evidence of the canal used to fill the reservoir. The best evidence was an eroded area with stacked stones containing a Pueblo I potsherd.

Hand-placed rocks, possibly used for protection against erosion, were also found along the bank upstream from Box Elder Reservoir, adding credence to the theory that this spot was a probable location for an intake canal. No evidence was found of a diversion structure near the point where a canal with a slope of 1 percent would intersect with Prater Canyon. No data were available for computing the intake canal capacity, and we therefore assumed that it was similar to the Morefield canal, with a capacity of about 19 cubic feet per second. This would appear reasonable based on a bottom width of 2 to 3 feet and would be somewhat greater than an estimated two-year flood peak of 5 cubic feet per second for Prater Canyon.

Table 7.1
Summary of Box Elder Reservoir Phases

Phase*	Description	Elevation	Approximate Time Period
I	Excavation of a pond to ground-water level west of the canyon thalweg. Collection of agricultural field runoff likely.	7,247	A.D. 800**
II	Deepening of the pond to 7,231 feet as the water table was lowered due to thalweg erosion that reduced the water table.	7,247	A.D. 825
III	Opening of the east bank of the reservoir to the canyon thalweg so water could flow in by gravity without an inlet canal.	7,242–7,245	A.D. 840
IV	Incomplete dredging operations, coupled with canyon thalweg degradation, required a short diversion canal.	7,239.5 (canal invert)	A.D. 850
V	The reservoir bottom rising up above the 7,240-foot level resulted in formal berm building and inlet canal extensions.	7,240+	A.D. 875
VI	Inlet canal extensions, finally to a route defined by canal stones.	7,249	A.D. 900
VII	Abandonment of inlet canal from thalweg and reliance on field runoff and west gully.	7,250.5	A.D. 925
VIII	Total abandonment.	7,251	A.D. 950

* Phasing estimates based on detailed geomorphologic findings and estimates prepared by Ernest Pemberton and John Rold.
** The initial excavation could have been started earlier when the valley thalweg was defined by the sloping no. 1 early terraces at elevation 7,247.

Reservoir Sedimentation

The reservoir cross-sections R A-A′ and R B-B′, shown in Figures 7.8 and 7.9, were based on extensive augering and drill-hole data; reservoir size estimates were based on surveying, USGS quad sheets, and detailed studies of Morefield Reservoir. The outer limits of the reservoir are in the form of an ellipse. The sediment volume accumulated in the storage area formed by a circular bottom, elliptical top, and a depth of 19 feet is about 152,000 cubic

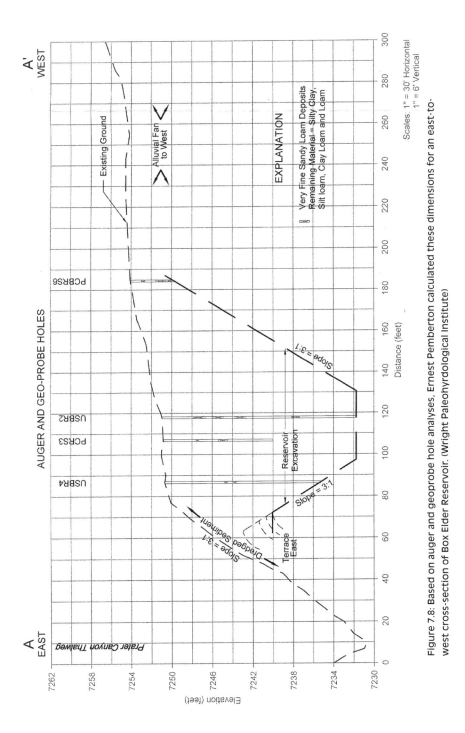

Figure 7.8: Based on auger and geoprobe hole analyses, Ernest Pemberton calculated these dimensions for an east-to-west cross-section of Box Elder Reservoir. (Wright Paleohyrdological Institute)

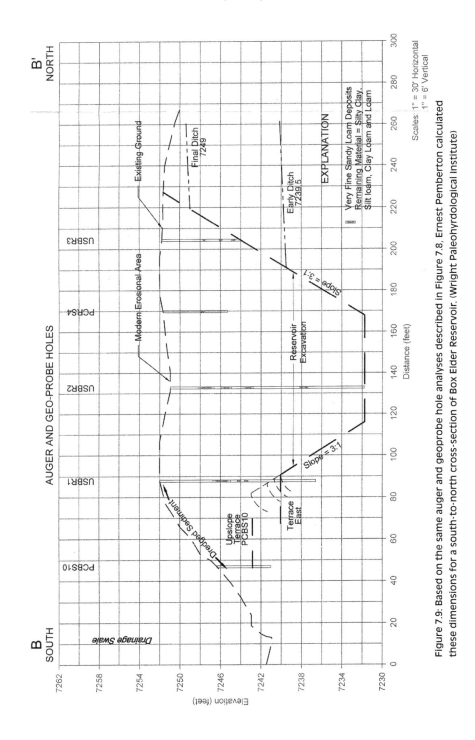

Figure 7.9: Based on the same auger and geoprobe hole analyses described in Figure 7.8, Ernest Pemberton calculated these dimensions for a south-to-north cross-section of Box Elder Reservoir. (Wright Paleohyrdological Institute)

feet. The 19-foot depth was determined by subtracting 1 foot from the total 20-foot depth to account for more postoperational surface deposits.

Using the figure of 152,000 cubic feet for sediment volume, the sediment yield for the nearly 4-square-mile drainage basin over a 150-year period would be about 0.0058 acre-foot per square mile per year. This yield is comparable to the Morefield Reservoir annual yield of 0.0067 acre-foot per square mile. Some of the sediment yield of Prater Canyon would bypass any diversion structure, and there are some unaccountable dredged materials dumped outside the reservoir storage area. Factoring in these unknowns, we estimated an annual prehistoric sediment yield of 0.01 acre-foot per square mile for Prater Canyon.

Prater Canyon Characteristics

Figure 7.3 shows geomorphologic cross-sections of the canyon. Figure 7.4 shows the geomorphologic mapping in plan view. In studying the channel hydraulics and valley bottom characteristics for Prater Canyon, we learned much through comparison with our earlier studies in Morefield Canyon. The two drainage basins, in addition to paralleling each other, had somewhat similar drainage areas of about 4 square miles and contained similar vegetation. Both had been free of forest fires for a hundred years or more. Also, the same geological formations occur upstream in both basins.

May 2003 groundwater investigations yielded no existing evidence of an easily accessible groundwater source for the Pueblo I and Pueblo II cultures in Prater Canyon. However, park historic water resources reports identified a few springs and were consistent with our team's opinion of an accessible groundwater table depth. Thick peat moss deposits in the upper canyon indicate extended periods of significant wetland deposits. Sustained drought periods not only affect the hydrology of surface water, and thus limit the availability of pocket water and seeps, but, in combination with fire, may also cause regional groundwater table lowering. The likelihood of prehistoric groundwater availability is supported by the Mesa Verde National Park data for the location of the springs plotted on Figure 7.10.

Potsherd Analysis

Southwest pottery expert David Breternitz performed an inventory of the ceramics at the site during Wright Paleohydrological Institute's October 2002 visit. His tabulation of inventoried ceramics is provided in Table 7.2.

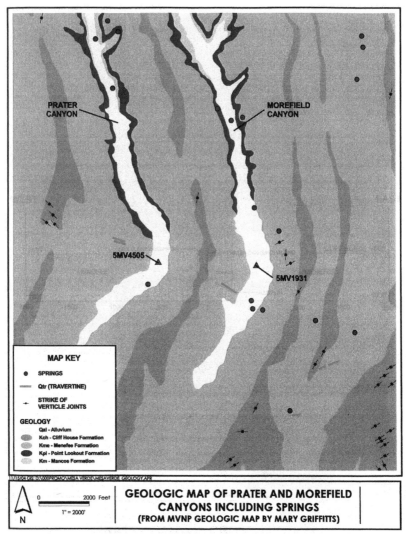

Figure 7.10: Mary Griffits, longtime Mesa Verde geologist, provided this assessment of the underlying geology of the Morefield and Prater Canyon area, along with the location of springs. (Wright Paleohyrdological Institute)

Dr. Breternitz concluded that the prehistoric ceramics at the Box Elder site were primarily from the Pueblo I period (A.D. 750–900). About 8 percent of the shards were from the Pueblo II period (A.D. 900–1100). Most of the ceramic shards were from jar-shaped vessels probably used to transport water from Box Elder Reservoir to nearby pueblos. They were found eroding from the reservoir's berm. No shards were found in the

			Table 7.2			
		Tabulation of Surface Ceramics, Site 5MV4505,				
		Prater Canyon, Mesa Verde National Park				
Type	**Jars**	**Rims**	**Bowls**	**Rims**	**Total**	**Percentage**
Chapin Black-on-White	—	—	1	—	1	1%
Piedra Black-on-White	—	—	1	—	1	1%
Mancos Black-on-White	1	—	—	1	2	2%
Whiteware	8	—	—	—	8	8%
Chapin Gray	—	1	—	1	2	2%
Moccasin Gray	3	1	—	—	4	4%
Early Pueblo Gray	70*	—	—	—	70	72%
"Corrugated"	6	—	—	—	6	6%
Fugitive Red	1	—	—	—	1	1%
Redware	2	—	—	—	2	2%
Totals	91	2	2	2	97	99%

* Two are jar handles.

auger holes. Based on the composition of the sample and its distribution, Breternitz concluded that the Box Elder Reservoir was in use from about A.D. 800 to about A.D. 950.

Breternitz also noted that most of the shards were Grayware as opposed to Whiteware and that they were similar to those found at Far View and Morefield Reservoirs. This suggests that Box Elder Reservoir was not used to any significant extent during the Pueblo II period. Most of the Pueblo II shards were on top of the mound and highest in the sediments, and likely represent activity from nearby Pueblo II residents and people living in a major pueblo about 0.5 mile down Prater Canyon from the Box Elder site.

Box Elder Reservoir in a Nutshell

In summary, Box Elder Reservoir is a 14-foot-high mound containing about 20 feet of sediment that is the remains of a Pueblo I/early Pueblo II reservoir. Our team determined that the reservoir began as an excavated pond for accessing groundwater in the Prater Canyon floor adjacent to, and lower than, the thalweg. The time was likely A.D. 800 or earlier. The canyon-bottom terraces were gently sloping all the way to the thalweg.

From time to time sediment entered the pond, which by that time had been excavated. As the water table dropped over time, the pond was deepened, finally to an elevation of 7,231 feet. Water was also collected from agricultural fields, as shown by the fact that the sediment contained maize pollen from upstream agricultural fields. Over time the pond bottom began to increase in elevation, and the water table was only periodically available in the pond bottom. The east bank of the reservoir was opened to the canyon thalweg for intermittent flows.

Later, because of its rise in elevation, the pond required a diversion canal from the Prater Canyon runoff for water supply. Sediment was continually deposited in the reservoir, and it was regularly dredged to help form the U-shaped berm.

Many reservoir subphases occurred over time as the reservoir bottom rose in elevation about 20 feet and the excavated material was used to create a berm. With each later phase, the inlet diversion canal was rebuilt and its point of diversion was extended upstream. Over a long period of time, about 150 years, the reservoir became elevated, the canal became longer, and the work required (for operation and maintenance) became greater for every gallon of water stored.

In the final stages of the reservoir, during the early Pueblo II period, the diversion canal from the thalweg of Prater Canyon was abandoned, and filling of the reservoir was shifted exclusively to the two minor tributary gulches that infrequently flowed from west to east down the canyon wall and from the agricultural fields. This phenomenon is evidenced by the higher-elevation sediment deposits lying on the west portion of the mound. Limited use of the storage site might have existed beyond A.D. 950, but not for very long. After abandonment of the reservoir, the sloping surface of the reservoir sediments experienced some west-to-east erosion.

Supplementing the reservoir water supply was the likely use of excavations in the canyon-bottom floor that reached the water table, though no evidence of such activity exists. Even today areas exist with occasional rather shallow water tables, as evidenced by intermittent lush vegetation adjacent to the Prater Canyon thalweg and historic homestead water wells of modest depths.

Similarities between the Box Elder Reservoir and Morefield Reservoir are significant. Similarly, the Pueblo I and Pueblo II occupational characteristics bear many similarities to Morefield Canyon, though the Prater Canyon population density may have been only 60 percent of that of

Morefield Canyon. The two reservoirs are on the same east-west latitude, as are the main pueblo areas.

Box Elder Reservoir would have been able to store water four or five times per year from the Prater Canyon watershed as it existed during the Pueblo I period. This was more than adequate to justify the human effort in building and maintaining the water supply structure.

People continued to live near Box Elder Reservoir after its abandonment.

8

Prehistoric Vegetation at Mesa Verde

THE INTERESTING AND IMPORTANT branch of science that is palynology represents the study of pollen and spores, whether living or dead. To us, palynology meant that we had an additional window into prehistory: a chance to find out about early farming near the reservoirs and even the rise and decline of prehistoric pine and juniper forests, the occurrence of wetland plants that might have grown in the reservoirs, and medicinal plants available to the early inhabitants of the area.

At each of the four reservoir sites we collected two types of soil samples that would be submitted to the palynology laboratory. First samples were collected from the land upstream of the reservoir where inspection indicated likely agricultural sites. The second type of samples were from the reservoir deposits, and here we typically collected a profile series from top to bottom. For two reservoirs, however, we collected the soil samples only from the perimeter waste-disposal zone where the dredged sediments had been dumped. Earlier investigations at these two sites had collected and interpreted pollen samples from the interior.

Plant Variety

The laboratory results were startling in their detail and what they told us. The frequent and sometimes abundant maize pollen retrieved from the reservoirs meant that intensive agriculture had taken place upstream from each of the reservoirs. We know this because maize pollen is not easily transported by wind but is readily transported by water, which was the vehicle for transport of the maize pollen grains into the reservoirs, where they became embedded in the sediment layers.

We also found pollen from typical riparian vegetation, such as cattail, smartweed, knotweed, phaselia, sedges, the buttercup family, and the pink family, even though such pollen was mostly absent from the upstream soil samples. This indicated that the reservoirs and inlet canals could support water-loving plants, perhaps along the perimeter of the water storage area. At Far View Reservoir, for instance, the pollen record presents a picture of plants that included tall cattails and short herbaceous plants growing in the mud at the edges of the reservoir while it contained water.

The palynology laboratories that performed these analyses are listed in Table 8.1.

There was a wide variety of pollen types found as part of the reservoir research studies. Table 8.2 is a list of typical pollen types with the scientific name paralleled with the common name given for each of the arboreal pollen, nonarboreal pollen, starches, and spores.

Morefield Reservoir

Eighteen soil samples were subjected to palynology analysis. The analysis of two of the six samples from the upstream agricultural area provided evidence of maize pollen. From a reservoir vertical profile, a total of twelve palynology samples were analyzed. We determined that there was evidence of abundant pine, juniper, and spruce forest. Unlike the palynological evidence on Chapin Mesa that indicated that the forests were being denuded, the evidence here indicated that Morefield Canyon maintained substantial arboreal resources. Of the more than fifty types of pollen identified, there were eight different types of trees as well as sunflowers, wetland plants, and beans.

Zea (maize) pollen, found in all twelve reservoir samples, provided additional evidence of maize agriculture upstream of the reservoir. In fact, there was a great deal of maize farming in Morefield Canyon. *Artemisia* (sagebrush) was common and abundant during the entire period, and *Ephedra* (Mormon tea) pollen was found in all samples (Figure 8.7).

Abundant charcoal was observed in all samples. Higher concentrations of pollen existed in clay deposits than in sand, likely because the clay was deposited in the reservoir much more slowly and, therefore, a given sample of clay represented a longer time period.

Table 8.1	
Palynology Laboratories Who Performed Analyses	
Reservoir Analyzed	**Laboratory**
Morefield	Paleo Research Laboratories
Far View	Paleo Research Institute
Sagebrush	Paleo Research Laboratories
Box Elder	Department of Geosciences at University of Arizona and Quaternary Services

Table 8.2
Summary of Pollen Types Found at Reservoir Sites

Scientific Name	Common Name
Arboreal pollen	
Carya	hickory, pecan
Juniperus	juniper
Pinaceae	pine family
Abies	fir
Picea	spruce
Pinus	pine
Pseudotsuga	Douglas fir
Quercus Sp	oak (Figure 8.2)
Nonarboreal pollen	
Asteraceae	sunflower family (Figure 8.3)
Artemisia	sagebrush
Cirsium	thistle
Low spine	includes ragweed, cocklebur, etc.
High spine	includes aster, rabbitbrush, snakeweed, sunflower, etc.
Liguliflorae	pollen morphological group, fenestrate type pollen
Cactaceae	cactus family
Cylindropuntia	cholla
Opuntia	prickly pear cactus (Figure 8.4)
Caryophyllaceae	pink family
Cheno-Am	includes amaranth and pigweed family
Sarcobatus vermiculatus	greasewood
Cleome	beeweed
Ephedra	Mormon tea
Ephedra navadensis-Type	Mormon tea
Ephedra torreyena-Type	Mormon tea
Fabaceae	bean or legume family
Onagraceae	evening primrose family (Figure 8.5)
Poaceae	grass family
Polygonaceae	knotweed/smartweed family
Eriogonum	wild buckwheat
Polygonum	knotweed
Polygonum sawaatchense	Sawatch knotweed
Ranunculaceae	buttercup family
Rosaceae	rose family (Figure 8.6)
Shepherdia	buffaloberry
Zea Mays	maize, corn
Indeterminate	too badly deteriorated or corroded to identify
Starches	
Oval, extra large, with linear hilum and an "x" under cross-polar illumination	potato-type
Spores	
Monolete	fern
Selaginella densa	little clubmoss
Triletefern	
Sporormiella	dung fungus

Far View Reservoir

At Far View we had the advantage of an earlier pollen analysis of two profiles from 1973 collected by David Breternitz from the interior of the structure. Only two grains of maize pollen were found in the twenty-two samples, both from near the bottom.

Based on this information, our 1999 reservoir soil samples were taken from between the two perimeter walls where the prehistoric dredged material was dumped. Here we hit a bonanza and recovered a lot of maize pollen and abundant wetland plant pollen. The arboreal pollen variations illustrated a picture of ancient environmental changes. We identified the drainage basin agricultural fields upstream with maize pollen.

Sagebrush Reservoir

Pollen sampling at Sagebrush was the source of this reservoir's name. We examined two sediment samples from a potential agricultural area and one from between the walls of the reservoir in 2001. *Artemisia* was the dominant species, along with members of the sunflower family and small amounts of *Zea mays* (maize) between the walls, as shown in Sample No. 3. The presence of pollens from moisture-loving plants supports the fact that

Figure 8.1: The paleohydrology team was pleased and proud to have Calvin Cummings, who had previously served as chief archaeologist for the National Park Service, on the team at Far View Reservoir. Here, he labels an important pollen soil sample prior to laboratory analysis. (Ruth Wright)

Figure 8.2: Oak. (Ken Wright)

Figure 8.3: Sunflower. (Ken Wright)

Figure 8.4: Prickly Pear. (Ken Wright)

Figure 8.5: Evening Primrose. (Ken Wright)

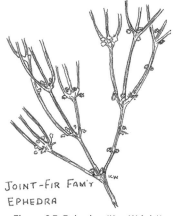

Figure 8.6: Chokecherry. (Ken Wright)

Figure 8.7: Ephedra. (Ken Wright)

the site was a reservoir. One badly preserved pollen grain points to the presence of cotton at the site, but this may have been due to some other phenomenon such as importation by trade.

Box Elder Reservoir

Samples from likely agricultural sites and the reservoir were taken in October 2002 and May 2003. The assemblage was dominated by *Pinus* (pine) and heavy with sunflower family pollens.

Although 2002 testing did not produce much *Zea mays* pollen, 2003 samples showed abundant maize pollen in two deep reservoir sediment columns. The maize pollen was carried into the reservoir sediments from upstream agricultural fields. Of the forty-one samples in 2003, thirty-five were from the reservoir and six from high up on the canyon walls, where no maize was found.

9

Technology Transfer

ONE OF THE ADVANTAGES of a systematic paleohydrological research effort spanning eleven years and four prehistoric projects was the opportunity to compare construction and management techniques. What we found surprised even our team archaeologists. The field evidence demonstrated remarkable similarities between the reservoir structures on the mesa tops and in canyon bottoms, in terms of both their building and operation. Remarkably, all four reservoirs lie on a common east-west line.

Similarities of the Mesa-Top Structures

There were many similarities between the two adjacent mesa-top reservoirs, Far View and Sagebrush Reservoirs:

- Both are located on narrow mesas;
- Both are located in areas of 2 percent slopes, just downstream from 3 percent slopes;
- Both are hindered by not having natural tributary water areas;
- Without human intervention, little harvested water would reach either reservoir;
- They are roughly the same size;
- They are roughly the same shape: one circular and one D-shaped;
- They both have double stone walls that partially ring the reservoir;
- They both have formal entranceways;
- Both have pond area stepping-stones to help in gathering water;
- Neither could be drained by gravity; that is, there are no outlets;
- Both have shallow bedrock at about 4–5 feet;
- Both have evidence of prehistoric dredging;
- The dredged material dumped in the areas between the stone walls provided maize pollen evidence;
- Both contained potsherds within the profile, though Sagebrush Reservoir had three sterile strata;
- Both are adjacent to pueblo dwelling units; and
- Both structures are estimated to be primarily Pueblo II, with Far View Reservoir ranging from A.D. 950–1180 and Sagebrush Reservoir from A.D. 950–1100.

111

Similarities of the Valley Structures

The visual similarities of Box Elder Reservoir and Morefield Reservoir are best illustrated by the fact that James Kleidon immediately judged the Prater Canyon mound to be a reservoir after seeing it from the mesa bare of sagebrush (Figure 9.1). Similarities between the two valley bottom reservoirs are numerous:

- The reservoirs were in adjacent canyons with drainage basins that were similar in terms of area slope, length, vegetation, and elevation;
- Both originated as excavated ponds on the valley floor.
- Sediment inflow that needed to be cleaned out was deposited in both reservoirs, but not all of the sediment could be removed from the bottom through dredging.
- Dredged sediment cast off to the perimeter of both reservoirs tended to create berms. With each cleaning, the berms grew in height and width.
- Following the early phase of the water storage, water would not flow into the reservoirs by gravity. In both cases, an inlet canal was necessary that would be periodically raised and extended upstream.
- Water from both reservoirs was collected mostly using ceramic jars, as evidenced by the potsherds analysis.
- The main occupied areas were about a half-mile downstream of the two reservoirs on a southeast-facing slope, well away from the canyon

Figure 9.1: Box Elder Reservoir is shown in the center of the photograph in the bottom of Prater Canyon. The view is looking north across the burn area of the 2000 Bircher Forest Fire. (Ruth Wright)

bottomlands that would have been used for agriculture. The pueblos in both canyons were not easily defensible.

- Sediment layering in both structures showed alternating strata of sandy accumulation and silt-clay deposits. Both contained iron staining and redoximorphic deposits that indicated standing water.
- Both sites are immediately adjacent to canyon valley-bottom channels.
- There was an overlapping period of reservoir use of approximately 150 years, A.D. 750–1100 in one instance and A.D. 800–950 in the other.
- Both reservoirs would have provided only a periodic domestic water supply due to the sporadic nature of the runoff events.
- The silt-clay reservoir deposits from routine runoff events were impermeable, and reservoir seepage would have been minor.
- Both reservoirs relied upon human-altered land use conditions related to deforestation (wood collection for fuel and building) coupled with agriculture in the valley bottomlands. Both drainage basins had occasional forest fires (fourteen in Morefield Canyon,) the effects of which might have lasted for ten to twenty years.

Comparing the Canyon-Bottom and Mesa-Top Reservoirs

The two mesa-top reservoirs were commenced some 150 to 200 years after the two valley-bottom reservoirs. It is likely that the mesa-top dwellers recognized the hydrological acumen of their neighbors some 5 miles to the east, even though they did not have any natural drainage basins to yield water for their structures. It would have been evident to the mesa-top people that water runoff could be carried and directed in open ditches to a reservoir. The mesa tops were covered with wind-deposited soils rich in silt and clay but with some sand fractions.

Maintenance of the reservoirs by dredging was common to all four reservoirs, especially Far View. All four had pueblo settlements within easy walking distance, and the people used ceramic jars for water transport (Figure 9.2). The women who would have collected the water for household use from the reservoirs occasionally dropped their jars or broke them in use, which resulted in the potsherds found at each site. For instance, at Morefield Reservoir 91 percent of the potsherds that could be classified came from jars, mostly utilitarian Pueblo II San Juan Whiteware. At Box Elder Reservoir 94 percent were from jars, mostly Early Pueblo Gray.

Figure 9.2: All of the reservoirs analyzed contained potsherds that helped to date the years of operation and to help establish the sites as reservoirs. Nearly all the potsherds were from jars. (Ken Wright)

10

Remarkable Legacy

WHEN SCHOLARS DESCRIBE the early citizens of Colorado and theorize about community development, too often they forget about the Ancestral Puebloans and their predecessors of the Basketmaker II period. They shouldn't!

Although reservoir operations at Mesa Verde lasted a long time and over many generations, until A.D. 1180, people inhabited Mesa Verde until about A.D. 1300—the period from A.D. 1100–1300 being the Pueblo III period, when there was a general movement from pueblos to cliff dwellings (Figure 10.1).

The reason reservoir building and operations generally ceased with the Pueblo II people is not known. However, these projects required considerable time and effort, along with extraordinary organizational skill to keep workers on the job. As the reservoirs got older, higher, and more difficult to operate, the labor input per gallon of water stored and used increased. For

Figure 10.1: Following the Pueblo I and II periods, conditions in Mesa Verde National Park changed enough that the Ancestral Puebloans began abandoning the mesa-top and canyon-bottom pueblos to move into cliff dwellings. Cliff dwellings represent the succeeding Pueblo III period of Mesa Verde that lasted until A.D. 1300. (Ken Wright)

this reason, one could imagine that the inhabitants would finally abandon a particular site and turn more to groundwater in the valley-bottom alluvium and the use of a few natural springs such as those at Spruce Tree House and Balcony House or the internal seepage at Cliff Palace.

The later people of Mesa Verde did not have an easy life. One of the worst droughts within the dendroclimate record, which goes all the way back to about A.D. 500 at Mesa Verde, started in A.D. 1135 and ran to A.D. 1180 (Figure 10.2). It was so widespread that even the central United States still bears the scars. For instance, in eastern Colorado, along the South Platte River near Hillrose, drought-induced sand dunes that originated in the mid-twelfth century still exist. In A.D. 1275 another drought struck that lasted until A.D. 1300.

Community

The people of southwestern Colorado left their mark on the area in the form of archaeological sites (Figures 10.3 and 10.4) that make us, in some ways, richer and smarter.

We are richer knowing that community development in Colorado extends back three thousand years. We are smarter because the Ancestral Puebloans' reservoirs have left a record of varying vegetation, of periods of drought and high-water flows, and even of forest fires. We are also enriched by knowing that the terrible drought of the twelfth century did not destroy community life or drive the Ancestral Puebloans out of Mesa Verde, even though they left later, between A.D. 1250 and 1300.

Figure 10.2: Pueblo Bonito in New Mexico's Chaco Canyon, by Richard Kern, artist and topographer with the U.S Topographical Engineers, 1849. The pueblo was abandoned in A.D. 1130. (Richard Kern)

Figure 10.3: This photograph of Spruce Tree House is from Mary Elizabeth Jane Colter's collection of early photographs of Mesa Verde. The woman on the ladder is believed to be Ms. Colter (1869–1958). (National Park Service)

Figure 10.4: The site of the Cliff Palace was selected for its environmental character, water seep, exposure, defensibility, and proximity to the canyon floor. It is, in some ways, like a modern apartment-building complex. (Gary Witt)

Reservoir Sediment Records

The records in the reservoir sediments provide irrefutable evidence that these water operations were continuous, over a period of as much as 350 years in one instance. The evidence also tells us about apparent remarkable achievements in social structure and organization. Otherwise, how could people be expected to operate, dredge, and maintain such huge public works projects over a span of fifteen to twenty generations?

The prehistoric data represented by alternating layers of clay and sand, potsherds, tools, ash layers, berm shapes, dredging activity and dumping areas, the curves of berm shaping and even a classic berm slope failure, and a layer of sand with ripples formed by a southwest wind provide clear and undisturbed evidence of daily activities. The sediments extend from bottom to top in a vertical sequence according to time; each year's deposit is on top of that of the previous year.

The mounds will be there for centuries to come. This means that a wealth of data exists at Mesa Verde for more detailed, but unhurried, study of these ancient peoples.

Water harvesting. By comparing present-day natural hydrological conditions in the canyons and on mesa tops with evidence of ancient water harvesting, we can estimate land surface modifications in prehistoric times. Agriculture, forest fires, heavily trodden footpaths, and packed areas near pueblos provided runoff from rainfall that far exceeded present-day conditions. These prehistoric runoff characteristics can be readily duplicated in the field. We learned that the Ancestral Puebloan people created water runoff where, now, one would expect there to be none.

Industriousness. Just how the Pueblo I people in Morefield Canyon could build a great kiva at the same time that they operated Morefield Reservoir between A.D. 750 and 1100 is a challenge to the imagination. This is especially true because there was also the need for hunting, farming, cutting wood for fuel, and building pueblos. The people must have stretched their human resources to the limit. They were diligent workers.

Security. Living in the canyon bottoms and on flat mesa tops near the reservoirs meant that there was little protection against organized marauders, yet this was how the Mesa Verde people lived from A.D. 750 to about 1100. Their occupation, in the later years, coincided with the Chaco Canyon influence throughout a large area of the southwest. With the demise of the settlements at Chaco, the period of moving to the defensible cliff houses in Mesa Verde tended to begin, perhaps by coincidence but possibly because the cliff dwellings provided more security.

The openness of the Pueblo I and II villages near the reservoir sites tells us that security was not a major problem at that time. It would appear that this was not the case in the Pueblo III times of cliff dwellings, many of which had ingenious and difficult in-and-out pathways of toe- and hand-holds and narrow passages.

Density of human population. Three of the four reservoir sites had a significant density of village occupancy nearby. The densest population in all of Mesa Verde was close to Morefield Reservoir. Far View Village, Pipe Shrine House, and Coyote Village on Chapin Mesa near Far View Reservoir also represented dense populations, as did the pueblos near Box Elder Reservoir. These three reservoirs were certainly important in terms of community development and water supply.

Agriculture. The reservoir research has told us much about Ancestral Puebloan agriculture and the use of medicinal plants and herbs. The evidence is there in the sediments, year by year, as the pollen was carried into the reservoirs and then preserved in the particular sediment layer that was laid down in that year. We learned about maize farming at all four reservoir sites.

Forest fires. For modern forest fire professionals, the evidence of the occurrence of fourteen significant fires over the 350-year period provides data that cannot be derived in any other manner.

Flooding or high water. Where else but in reservoir sediments can one look at a record of several centuries with the evidence of flooding or high water laid out like an open book, a record that could be analyzed as to approximate time and even, to a degree, magnitude, and duration?

Sediment rates. The potential exists to study prehistoric erosion and sedimentation rates from known areas.

Technology. The reservoir archaeological sites tell us about canal-building technology over a period of more than a century. Cross-sections at Morefield showed canal after canal stacked up on top of each other. Thin sand and gravel deposits even showed what the canal looked like and provided opportunities to measure the width and depth of each canal that existed for decades more than one thousand years ago.

What Does This Mean?

The Mesa Verde reservoirs have provided a whole new picture of Ancestral Puebloan successes and daily activities during the period preceding the cliff dwellings. Unlike many archaeological artifacts in the areas of the cliff dwellings, the record has not been disturbed by looters because the evidence is all underground with little value. Future research and studies of the Ancestral Puebloans could take a new turn by focusing on the reservoir structures. By learning more about these ancient people, we can learn more about Colorado and ourselves.

Bibliography

Arrhenius, G., and E. Bonatti. 1965. The Mesa Verde Loess. In *Contributions of the Wetherill Mesa Archaeological Project,* ed. D. Osborne, 92–101. Memoirs of the Society for American Archaeology, No. 19. Washington, DC: Society for American Archaeology.

Breternitz, David A. 1999. *The 1969 Far View Reservoir Excavations, Site 5MV833.* Denver, CO: WPI.

Breternitz, D. A., A. H. Rohn, Jr., and E. A. Morris, eds. 1974. *Prehistoric Ceramics of the Mesa Verde Region.* Ceramic Series No. 5. Flagstaff: Museum of Northern Arizona.

Chapin, F. H. 1892. *The Land of the Cliff Dwellers.* Boston: W. B. Clark.

Collins, S. M. 2002. Letter to Kenneth R. Wright. October 28.

———. 1987. "Prehistoric and Historic Cultural Resources of Mesa Verde National Park." National Register of Historic Places Multiple Property Documentation Form.

Crown, P. L. 1987. Water Storage in the Prehistoric Southwest. *The Kiva* 52(3): 209–228.

Cummings, L. S. 2001. Pollen Analysis at Sagebrush Reservoir, 5MV1936, Colorado. Golden, CO: Paleo Research Laboratories.

———. 1999. Pollen Analysis of Far View Reservoir and the Far View Reservoir Drainage Basin, Mesa Verde, Colorado. Golden, CO: Colorado and Paleo Research Institute.

Cummings, L. S., and T. E. Moutoux. 1998. Exploratory Pollen Analysis of Two Samples from 5MV1931, Morefield Canyon, Colorado. Denver, CO. Paleo Research Laboratories.

Davis, O. K. 2003. "Analysis of Box Elder Reservoir 5MV4505—Mesa Verde, N.M." Department of Geosciences. University of Arizona. July 11.

Dean, J. S., and W. J. Robinson. 1977. *Climatic Variability in the American Southwest, A.D. 680 to 1970.* Tucson, AZ: Laboratory of Tree-Ring Research.

Erdman, J. A., C. L. Douglas, and J. W. Marr. 1969. *Environment of Mesa Verde, Colorado.* Archeological Research Series, No. 7B. Washington, DC: National Park Service.

Ferguson, W. M. 1996. *The Anasazi of Mesa Verde and the Four Corners.* Niwot: University of Colorado Press.

Fewkes, J. W. 1917. *A Prehistoric Mesa Verde Pueblo and Its People.* Smithsonian Report for 1916: 461–488. Washington, DC: Government Printing Office.

Griffitts, M. O. 1990. *Guide to the Geology of Mesa Verde National Park.* Mesa Verde National Park, CO: Mesa Verde Museum Association, Inc.

Haase, W. R. 1985. Domestic Water Conservation Among the Northern San Juan Anasazi. *Southwestern Lore* 50(2): 15–26.

Hayes, A. C. 1964. *The Archeological Survey of Wetherill Mesa, Mesa Verde National Park, Colorado.* Archeological Research Series, No. 7-A. Washington, DC: National Park Service.

Herold, J. L. 1961. *Prehistoric Settlement and Physical Environment in the Mesa Verde Area.* University of Utah Anthropological Papers, No. 53. Salt Lake City: University of Utah.

Hewitt, A. F., Jr. 1968. The Salvage Excavation of Site 1914, Navajo Canyon. In *Contributions to Mesa Verde Archaeology: V, Emergency Archaeology in Mesa Verde National Park, Colorado, 1948–1966*, ed. R. H. Lister, 37–44. University of Colorado Studies, Series in Anthropology, No. 15. Niwot: University of Colorado Press.

Holloway, R. G. 2003. *Pollen Analysis of Samples from 5MV4505, Box Elder Reservoir, Mesa Verde National Park, Colorado.* Quaternary Services Technical Report Series, Report No. 2003-23. October.

Hunt, C. B. 1956. *Cenozoic Geology of the Colorado Plateau.* USGS Professional Paper 279. Washington, DC: Government Printing Office.

Jennings, C. H. 1968. Salvage Excavations at Sites 1094 and 1093, East Fork of Navajo Canyon. In *Contributions to Mesa Verde Archaeology: V, Emergency Archaeology in Mesa Verde National Park, Colorado, 1948–1966*, ed. R. H. Lister, 45–52. University of Colorado Studies, Series in Anthropology, No. 15. Niwot: University of Colorado Press.

Kleidon, J. 2001. Post Fire Assessment—D018 (5MV4505) Field Notes.

Lancaster, J. 1969. *Far View Reservoir, Mesa Verde National Park, David A. Breternitz 1969 Excavations, Field Notes.* Typed from original field book by Ruth M. Wright at the Mesa Verde National Park Research Center, and verified by Jack E. Smith, July 21–23, 1998.

Leeper, J. W. 1986. A Computer Model of Far View Reservoir Water Collection System in Mesa Verde National Park. *Proceedings of the Sixth Annual American Geophysical Front Range Branch Hydrology Days.* Fort Collins: Colorado State University.

Lekson, S., Curtis P. Nepstad-Thornberry, Brian E. Yunker, Toni S. Laumbach, David P., and Karl W. Laumbach. 2002. "Migrations in the Southwest: Pinnacle Ruin, Southwestern New Mexico." *Kiva* 68(2): 73–101.

Lipe, W. D., M. D. Varien, and R. H. Wilshusen, eds. 1999. *Colorado Prehistory: A Context for the Southern Colorado River Basin.* Denver: Colorado Council of Professional Archaeologists.

Lister, R. H. 1964. *Contributions to Mesa Verde Archaeology: I, Site 499, Mesa Verde National Park, Colorado.* University of Colorado Studies, Series in Anthropology, No. 9. Niwot: University of Colorado Press.

———. 1965. *Contributions to Mesa Verde Archaeology: II, Site 875, Mesa Verde National Park, Colorado.* University of Colorado Studies, Series in Anthropology, No. 11. Niwot: University of Colorado Press.

———. 1966. *Contributions to Mesa Verde Archaeology: III, Site 866 and the Cultural Sequence at Four Villages in the Far View Group, Mesa Verde National*

Park, Colorado. University of Colorado Studies, Series in Anthropology, No. 12. Niwot: University of Colorado Press.

————. 1967. *Contributions to Mesa Verde Archaeology: IV, Site 1086, An Isolated, Above Ground Kiva in Mesa Verde National Park, Colorado*. University of Colorado Studies, Series in Anthropology No. 13. Niwot: University of Colorado Press.

Lister, R. H., and D. A. Breternitz. 1968. The Salvage Excavation of Site 1104, Wetherill Mesa. In *Contributions to Mesa Verde Archaeology: V, Emergency Archaeology in Mesa Verde National Park, Colorado, 1948–1966*, ed. R. H. Lister, 69–88. University of Colorado Studies, Series in Anthropology, No. 15. Niwot: University of Colorado Press.

Lucius, W., and D. A. Breternitz. 1981. The Current Status of Red Wares in the Mesa Verde Region. In *Collected Papers in Honor of Erik Kellerman Reed*, ed. A. H. Schroeder, 99–111. Papers of the Archaeological Society of New Mexico. Albuquerque: Archaeological Society of New Mexico.

Madole, R. F. 1995. Spatial and Temporal Patterns of Late Quaternary Eolian Deposition, Eastern Colorado, USA. *Quaternary Science Review* 14: 155–177.

Martin, P. S., and W. Byers. 1965. Pollen and Archaeology at Wetherill Mesa. In *Contributions of the Wetherill Mesa Archeological Project*, ed. Douglas Osborne, 122–135. Society for American Archeology Memoir 19. Washington, DC: Society for American Archeology.

Nordby, L. V. 2000. Letter to Kenneth R. Wright and Wright Water Engineers. January 19.

Nordenskiold, G. 1893. *The Cliff Dwellers of the Mesa Verde, Southwestern Colorado*. Translated by D. Lloyd Morgan. Stockholm: P. A. Norstedt and Soner.

Osborne, D. 1964. Solving the Riddles of Wetherill Mesa. *National Geographic* 125(2): 155–195.

Pemberton, E. L. 1997. Evaluation of May 1997 Field Trip, Site 5MV1931, Morefield Canyon.

Rohn, A. H. 1977. *Cultural Change and Continuity on Chapin Mesa*. Lawrence: University Press of Kansas.

————. 2003. Letter with manuscript comments. April 22.

————. 1963. Prehistoric Soil and Water Conservation on Chapin Mesa, Southwestern Colorado. *American Antiquity* 28(4): 441–455.

————. 1972. Social Implications of Pueblo Water Management in the Northern San Juan. *Zeitschrift für Ethnologie* 97: 212–219.

Rold, J. W. 1997. *Geology and Geomorphologic History of Morefield Canyon, Mesa Verde National Park, Montezuma County, Colorado*. Denver, CO: Mesa Verde Paleohydrologic Survey.

Scott, L. J. n.d. Palynological Investigations at 5MV1936. Golden, CO: Paleo Research Laboratories.

————. 1973. *Pollen Analysis of Far View Reservoir*. Golden, CO: Colorado and Paleo Research Institute.

Sheets, P. D., and T. C. Birkedal. 1968. Site 1107, a Small Pueblo II Unit on Wetherill Mesa. In *Contributions to Mesa Verde Archaeology: V, Emergency Archaeology in Mesa Verde National Park, Colorado, 1948–1966*, ed. R. H. Lister, 89–94. University of Colorado Studies, Series in Anthropology, No. 15. Niwot: University of Colorado Press.

Smith, J. E. 1987. *Mesas, Cliffs, and Canyons: The University of Colorado Archaeological Survey of Mesa Verde National Park*. Mesa Verde Research Series, Paper No. 3. Mesa Verde, CO: Mesa Verde Museum Association.

———. 1999. *The 1972 and 1974 Excavations of a Potential Prehistoric Reservoir (Site 5MV1936) Mesa Verde National Park, Colorado*. Boulder, CO: WPI.

———. 1979. A Re-evaluation of Prehistoric Water Control at Mesa Verde. Presented at Second Conference of Science in the National Park Service, San Francisco.

Smith, J. E., and E. Zubrow. 1999. *1967 Excavations at Site 5MV1931, Morefield Canyon, Mesa Verde National Park, Colorado*. Denver, CO: WPI

Stewart, G. R. 1940. Conservation in Pueblo Agricultural: I. Primitive Practices; II. Present-Day Flood Water Irrigation. *Scientific Monthly* 51(3–4): 201–220; 329–340.

Stewart, G. R., and M. Donnelly. 1943. Soil and Water Economy in the Pueblo Southwest. *The Scientific Monthly* 56 (January): 31–44 and 56 (February): 134–144.

U.S. Department of the Interior, Southern States Burned Area Emergency Rehabilitation Team. 2000. Bircher Fire Burned Area Emergency Rehabilitation (BAER) Plan.

Wanek, A. A. 1959. *Geology and Fuel Resources of the Mesa Verde Area, Montezuma and La Plata Counties, Colorado*. Geological Survey Bulletin 1072-M. Washington, DC: USGS.

Wenger, G. R. 1991. *The Story of Mesa Verde National Park*. Mesa Verde, CO: Mesa Verde Museum Association.

Weston, T. 1978. *The Archaeological Survey of Park Mesa, Mesa Verde National Park, Colorado*. Master's thesis, Department of Anthropology, University of Colorado, Boulder.

Wheat, J. B. 1952. Prehistoric Water Sources of the Point of Pines Area. *American Antiquity* 17(3): 186–196.

Wilshusen, R. M., M. J. Churchill, and J. M. Potter. 1997. Prehistoric Reservoirs and Water Basins in the Mesa Verde Region: Intensification of Water Collection Strategies During the Great Pueblo Period. *American Antiquity* 62(4): 664–681.

Woosley, A. I. 1980. Agricultural Diversity in the Prehistoric Southwest. *The Kiva* 45(4): 317–335.

Wright, K. R. 2000. *Paleohydrology Study of Far View Reservoir 1998–99, Site 5MV833*. Denver, CO: WPI.

———. 2003. "Water for the Anasazi: How the Ancients of Mesa Verde Engineered Public Works." *Essays in Public Works History, Number 22*. Kansas City, MO: Public Works Historical Society.

Wright, K. R., E. L. Pemberton, and J. E. Smith. 2001. Mesa Verde Prehistoric Reservoir Sedimentation. Presented at the Seventh Federal Interagency Sedimentation Conference, March 25–29, 2001, Reno, NV.

Wright Paleohydrological Institute. 2004. *Box Elder Reservoir Paleohydrology Site 5MV4505 Prater Canyon.* December. Denver, CO: WPI.

———. 2002. *Paleohydrology Sagebrush Reservoir Site 5MV1936.* Denver, CO: WPI.

———. 2002. *Progress Report—Box Elder Reservoir, 5MV4505 (a.k.a. D018).* Denver, CO: WPI.

Wright Water Engineers, Inc. 1998. *Final Report, Morefield Canyon Reservoir Paleohydrology, Mesa Verde National Park; Site 6MV1931.* Denver, CO: Wright Water Engineers, Inc.

Wyckoff, D. G. 1974. A Pollen Profile from Far View Reservoir, Mesa Verde National Park, Colorado. Anthropology 577. Pullman: Washington State University.

Appendix:

Geology and Geomorphology
of Morefield Canyon

Excerpted from Rold, J. W. 1997. *Geology and Geomorphologic History of More-field Canyon, Mesa Verde National Park, Montezuma County, Colorado.* Denver, CO: Mesa Verde Paleohydrologic Survey.

THE MESA VERDE plateau is held up by the sandstones of the Cretaceous age Mesaverde formation, which are more erosion resistant than the surrounding Mancos Shales. The top of the plateau is essentially a dip slope lying on the Cliff House Sandstone in the upper Mesaverde group (Figure A.1). The numerous north/south-trending canyons—of which Morefield Canyon is only one example—have cut through the Cliff House Sandstone and are floored in the sands and shales of the Menefee formation. The basal Point Lookout Sandstone only outcrops around the edges of the plateau. The gentle southward dip of the bedrock of 235 feet per mile (4.4 percent or approximately three degrees) into the San Juan Basin to the south only slightly exceeds the south slope of the valley floors.

Figure A.1. View of Morefield Canyon looking north.

The Recent or Holocene alluvium underlies the broad, flat valley floors. No bedrock outcrops were observed along the valley bottom. No data have been found to establish the thickness of the alluvium in Morefield Canyon. A simple projection of the valley wall profiles (Figure A.2) would indicate as much as 250 feet of alluvium. If the original, eroded bedrock were carved into a V-shaped canyon, this would be a reasonable estimate. Even if the original bedrock valley were flat-bottomed instead of V-shaped, one would expect the alluvium to be at least 100 feet thick.

No active erosion was observed (1997) in the floor of Morefield Canyon except at the few intermittent headcuts in the channel; even these appeared to be healing.

Each side or tributary canyon formed a gentle, rounded alluvial or debris fan extending onto, and sometimes almost across, the valley bottom. Each side canyon has a ready source of flagstone-like boulders. The jointing and bedding of the sandstone beds produce numerous platy sandstone boulders—usually of rectangular shape—one and a half to two feet long, one foot to 18 inches wide, and 2 inches to 6 inches thick. These flat boulders litter the valley walls and the floors of the side canyons. Either the side canyon storm runoff lacks sufficient energy to carry the large boulders onto the fans, or the boulders quickly disintegrate. Even a short distance from the

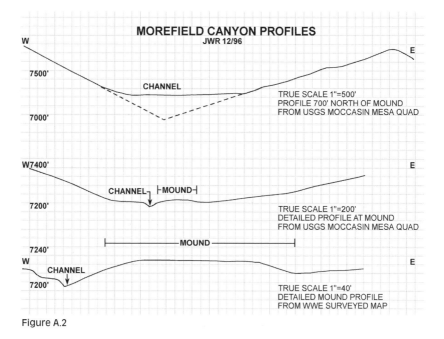

Figure A.2

canyon mouths, only cobble-sized boulders occur. Only 200 to 300 feet from the canyon mouths on the fans, only small cobbles and gravel-sized pebbles occur. Most of the fan material appears to be sand and clay.

Nowhere in Morefield Canyon were the gravels or cobbles of quartz, igneous rock, chert, or limestone commonly found in stream canyons in western Colorado observed. Doug Ramsey reported that no gravels had ever been found in the valleys of the Mesa Verde plateau. Although the 1959 U.S. Geological Survey map shows very sparse occasional occurrences of undated high-level terrace and pediment gravels on the mesa tops, none are indicated in the plateau's numerous valleys. This is important, because it proves a local provenance of the alluvium rather than a distant source from the mountains to the north. It also helps to date the age of the valleys and indicates that the valleys were probably beheaded prior to the Pleistocene when glacial outwash gravels were widely distributed in the stream channels leading from the mountains.

This lack of naturally deposited coarse-rock fragments in the valley alluvium has an important archeological connotation as well. It validates the concept that almost any rock of greater than cobble size would have to have been carried to its location.

Field observations indicate Morefield Canyon to be aggregating or filling rather than eroding. Erosion in the channel cannot carry away the load of material carried into the valley bottom by wind and by the slope wash and side canyon flows initiated by the occasional summer thunderstorms. Permeabilities appear high enough that snowmelt and moderate rains would seep into the ground rather than providing channel flows. The lack of a current erosional channel would appear to confirm this. Much of the deposition probably originates from wind erosion from the ridge tops and the bare valley walls. Whereas the canyons run north-south across the dominant wind direction, each canyon would trap airborne sediment somewhat like a giant snow fence.

Geologic and Geomorphic History

A description of the geologic and geomorphic history of Morefield Canyon is important in understanding natural phenomena that influenced reservoir building, its operation and maintenance. The geologic history pertinent to the Mesa Verde area began some 100 million years ago with the deposition of the marine Mancos Shale. As mountains rose to the west, the shoreline regressed northeastward across these marine shales. Behind and southwest of the shoreline, coal swamps were formed, and these sandstones, coals, and shales are now called the Mesaverde formation. After deposition of the Cliff House sands, the sea transgressed southwestward over the area depositing the Lewis Shale.

About 70 million years ago, as the San Juan and La Plata Mountains began to rise to the north and the San Juan Basin began to subside to the south, these Mesaverde beds were tilted southward to their present attitude. Erosion of materials from the mountains to the north and the stratigraphically younger beds above the Mesaverde formation formed the Animas and younger formations that now cap the San Juan Basin. Major drainage patterns of the San Juan, Animas, Mancos, and Dolores rivers and McElmo Creek developed in late Eocene and Miocene time. The larger through-going north/south valleys on the Mesa Verde plateau probably also developed at that time.

The headward erosion of the Mancos River, McElmo Creek, and their tributaries then eroded through the Mesaverde formation to the north of the present Mesa Verde plateau. As soon as the Mesaverde Sandstones were breached, erosion proceeded rapidly in the more-easily-eroded shales of the Mancos formation. The marked differential erosion and the capture and diversion of the streams that once flowed in the canyons on the plateau formed the topography we see today.

Ever since the canyons were beheaded by stream capture, significant through-going stream flow has not existed at Morefield Canyon, and the canyon has been slowly filling by aggradation. Thunderstorm sheet flow from the canyon walls and side canyon runoff furnish more clay and sand sediment to the valley than can be carried down the valley. The good permeability of the material and the flat valley gradient would inhibit runoff and contribute much of the snow melt and summer showers to the water table, which would probably be fairly shallow.

When the Mesa Verdeans settled the Morefield Canyon area, the valley bottom was probably a lush meadow with no developed drainage channel. The shallow water table may well have contributed to shallow springs or seeps. As the settlement grew over the many years of occupation, they would have required considerable area for growing food. Likely, most of the flat valley floor would have been converted from natural vegetation to the bare ground for their crops. This activity alone could easily have triggered an erosional cycle in the erodible soils of the valley bottom.

Trees on the valley slopes would have been removed as fuel for heating and cooking and for construction. These two man-caused activities (removal of the grass and shrubs in the valley bottoms and the removal of trees from the valley slopes) would have increased runoff and likely triggered erosion of the broad 40-foot to 60-foot-wide and 6-foot to 8-foot-deep channel now seen in the valley floor (Figures A.3 and A.4). This down-cutting would have lowered the water table, drying up most springs and seeps.

The anomalous drift of the Morefield Canyon channel noted by Pemberton (1997) may have resulted from the Mesa Verdeans' efforts to divert

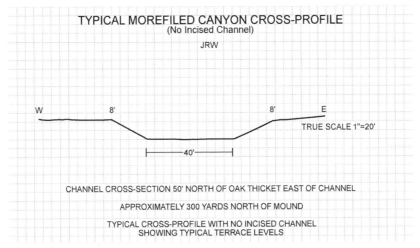

Figure A.3

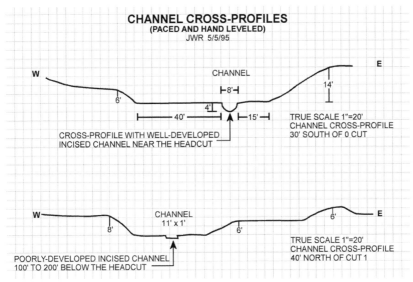

Figure A.4

the erosive drainage away from their fields. Another natural possibility could be that the debris fans from the east side of the valley crowded the drainage toward the west side of the valley.

Following abandonment of the reservoir and as grass and other native vegetation colonized the area, erosion would have ceased, and the channel would have healed to what we see in 1997. A similar triggering of an erosion cycle occurred in East Canyon, the valley immediately east of More-field, by the large Whites Mesa fire in the 1950s. The fire would have consumed all the vegetation and facilitated serious erosion. The bottom of East Canyon now has a fairly recent channel, estimated to be 30 to 50 years old. This channel is 10 to 20 feet wide and 10 to 15 feet deep. Grass now covers the burned slopes; erosion has slowed, and the channel is beginning to heal.

The several small discontinuous head-cuts noted in 1997 in Morefield Canyon may have started as a result of overgrazing in the early 1900s and the severe drought of the 1930s (Figure A.5). Several small check dams in these head-cut channels appear to have been built by the Civilian Conservation Corps in the late 1930s and early 1940s. These check dams and reduced grazing have reduced erosion, and the head cuts appeared to be healing until the Bircher Forest Fire in 2000.

Figure A.5. Valley bottom of Morefield Canyon near Morefield Reservoir.